Pause
and
Pray

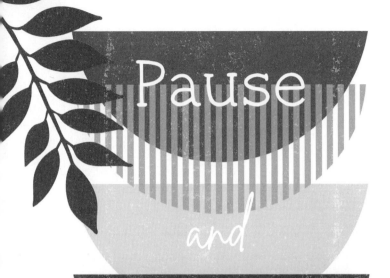

Pause and Pray

180 Encouraging Devotional Prayers for Women

BARBOUR
PUBLISHING

Pause. . .*and* Pray!

*Devote yourselves to prayer,
being watchful and thankful.*
COLOSSIANS 4:2 NIV

The all-powerful God cares deeply for you, even in the day-to-day details of your life. In fact, He longs to hear from you. You are invited—any time and for any reason—to bring any prayer to the King of the universe. Now that's genuine love!

The prayers in this book will help you develop a more intimate relationship with the heavenly Father. As you read the devotional prayers, make them your own. Meditate on the scriptures. You may even wish to keep a journal on hand to record your personal thoughts as you reflect upon God's amazing love for you.

You will be blessed when you pause and pray!

My Place of Quiet Peace

This world is so loud; it constantly shouts for my attention. My head fills up with so much stuff—things I need to do, questions I need to answer, and never-ending activity. The fast-paced merry-go-round of life won't stop, but I can step off. Help me remember to take time to slow down, to sit down and become quiet with You. Nowhere else do I experience the peace You provide. I need time with You every day. Help me to diligently spend those quiet moments with You. Let Your peaceful presence wash over me and quiet my soul.

||||||||||||||||||||||||||||||||||||||||||||||||||||||||||||||||||||

You're my place of quiet retreat;
I wait for your Word to renew me.
PSALM 119:114 MSG

Joy in the Name of the Lord

Father, this morning I meet You here for just a few moments before the busyness of the day takes over. I trust You. It is not always easy to trust, but You have proven trustworthy in my life. I find joy in the knowledge that You are my defender. You go before me this day into battle. I choose joy today because I love the name of the Lord Almighty. Amen.

|||||||||||||||||||||||||||||||||||||||||||||||||||||||||||||||||||||||||||||||||

But let all those that put their trust in thee rejoice:
let them ever shout for joy, because thou defendest them:
let them also that love thy name be joyful in thee.
PSALM 5:11 KJV

Be Still

Lord, You know it's hard for me to be still. I feel like I need to be doing something, but You have strongly encouraged me in Your Word to be still so that I might experience Your salvation. Help me rest in You. I open my heart and allow Your peace to comfort me. I will shut my mouth and listen as Your wisdom speaks to me. I stand in the quiet of Your presence and wait. Only You can defeat my enemies; only You can overcome the challenges I'm facing. I am calm, and obedient to Your voice. I wait with Your patience. You are fighting for me. I will be still and allow You to do a mighty work on my behalf.

‖‖

"The LORD is fighting for you! So be still!"
EXODUS 14:14 GW

A Godly Example

God, help me to be an example of a faithful disciple of Christ to my family and friends. Those who are close in our lives have the ability to lead us toward or away from righteousness and godliness. I pray that all I do and say will honor You and that I will never be a stumbling block to others. May all within my sphere of influence find me faithful to You. Amen.

|||||||||||||||||||||||||||||||||||||||||||||||||||||||||||||||||||||||||||

The righteous is more excellent than his neighbour:
but the way of the wicked seduceth them.
PROVERBS 12:26 KJV

He's in Control

Thank You, Lord, that You have a perfect plan for my life. I know I don't always understand it, but You know what's best, and everything that happens is for a reason—that You might be glorified. I'm so glad that You are in control and that I need not worry. Amen.

||||||||||||||||||||||||||||||||||||||||||||||||||||||||||||||||||||||||||||

There are many devices in a man's heart;
nevertheless the counsel of the LORD, that shall stand.
PROVERBS 19:21 KJV

Made in His Image

Lord, I know You created Eve with utmost care. She was the perfect pairing for Adam, crafted from his own body. But above this, Lord, I know Eve was formed in Your image. Before the Fall, Eve had no concept of beauty standards; she felt no inadequacy or unworthiness. All she knew was that she belonged to her Creator, and that was enough. It was only when sin entered the world that she became ashamed of herself. Ashamed of her body and her choices.

Father, I live in a world dominated by voices telling me what I should look like. It feels impossible to see myself the way You do—perfectly created for a purpose, made beautiful in the image of my Savior. Help me to be confident in the body You made for me and rejoice in what it can do for You. Amen.

||||||||||||||||||||||||||||||||||||||||||||||||||||||||||||||||||||||||||||||||

So God created mankind in his own image, in the image of God he created them; male and female he created them.
GENESIS 1:27 NIV

Keep My Footsteps Steady

Your Word is perfect, Your principles long-standing and proven over many lifetimes. You revive my soul with Your wise and trustworthy commands. They fill my heart with joy. My love for Your laws keeps my footsteps steady, and I am safe. Lord, help me discern my errors, and forgive my hidden faults. Keep me from willful sins so that they will not control my life. May the words of my mouth and the meditation of my heart be pleasing in Your sight. Thank You for steadying me in troubled times with the truth of Your Word.

The law of the Lord is perfect, converting the soul;
the testimony of the Lord is sure, making wise the simple;
the statutes of the Lord are right, rejoicing the heart;
the commandment of the Lord is pure, enlightening the eyes.
PSALM 19:7–8 NKJV

Delight God's Heart

Heavenly Father, I rejoice in my relationship with You. Today I offer the purest worship through thanksgiving. Thank You for the many undeserved blessings You bestow on me daily. You provide the air I breathe, the life I live, and the joy I experience. You hear my prayers always. I am grateful for Your presence; You are always near. I live my life today in absolute surrender to You. You have given me life, and I give my life back to You. I am filled with awe at the opportunity to do life together.

|||||||||||||||||||||||||||||||||||||||||||||||||||||||||||||||||||||||||

*Since we are receiving our rights to an unshakable
kingdom we should be extremely thankful and offer
God the purest worship that delights his heart as we lay
down our lives in absolute surrender, filled with awe.*
HEBREWS 12:28 TPT

Breathe Prayers

You tell me in Your Word to remain in an atmosphere of prayer. You are always with me, and I want to be listening every moment. Please fill my heart and mind with a desire to stay in communication with You throughout my day. Tune my heart to hear You. May Your Spirit flow through me just like the air I breathe in and out. Let my thoughts be on the work You have for me to do. Fill me with compassion for others. May my lips be ready to speak Your truth in love to those around me, but give me wisdom to know when to be quiet and breathe out a prayer instead.

|||||||||||||||||||||||||||||||||||||||||||||||||||||||||||||||||||||||||

"The Spirit of God made me what I am,
the breath of God Almighty gave me life!"
JOB 33:4 MSG

14

Choosing Joy, Peace, and Hope

Father, fill my heart with the absolute joy of Your presence today. Fill me with the peace of Your nature and the unwavering hope for my future. Everywhere I look, it seems I can always find a reason to doubt Your goodness and Your omnipotence. Forgive me for the way I have turned from You in moments of uncertainty. I choose, Lord, to start new and to see these complications as opportunities to trust in You.

I am confident in the joy, peace, and hope You give me through the Holy Spirit. Your unlimited power resides in my heart. Help me access that power to see Your hand in every situation from the wonderful to the heartbreaking. Amen.

|||||||||||||||||||||||||||||||||||||||||||||||||||||||||||||||||||||||||||||

*May the God of hope fill you with all joy and peace
as you trust in him, so that you may overflow
with hope by the power of the Holy Spirit.*
ROMANS 15:13 NIV

Put Me Back Together

Sometimes life brings wonderful and amazing things from You. Other times I find myself in a battle that I'm losing. On the days I want to quit, I know I can't. I am reminded that no matter how painful the situation or how broken I am, I am committed to You. Even when I feel like I've lost myself, with pieces of my heart scattered all over the place, somehow You find me and put me back together with Your Word. Whisper Your truth to me. I will never forsake Your way! I adhere my heart tightly to Your sayings. Your constant love renews me with the strength I need.

||||||||||||||||||||||||||||||||||||||||||||||||||||||||||||||||||||||||||

I've committed myself and I'll never turn back from living by your righteous order. Everything's falling apart on me, GOD; put me together again with your Word.
PSALM 119:106–107 MSG

In the Waves

Lord, I am like Peter walking to You on the waves. You tell me to take courage and to not be afraid. You tell me to come to You, and I step out of my boat of comfort, of stability. I am so confident and sure of Your power until I focus on the darkness around me, the heartache, and my own sin. Before I know it, I falter. I sink faster every moment I don't trust Your ways.

Forgive me for taking my eyes off You. Forgive me for trying to do things on my own instead of letting You lead. I thank You for always catching me when I fall, for pulling me from the water and the waves of life. Today, Lord, I ask You to help me rely on the truth that I can stand firm in my faith during storms because You are for me.

| | | | | | | | | | | | | | | | | | | | | | | | | | | | | | | | | | | | | | | | | | | | | | | | | | | | | | | | | | | |

Immediately Jesus reached out his hand and caught him. "You of little faith," he said, "why did you doubt?"
MATTHEW 14:31 NIV

17

Showing Mercy

Jesus, like the good Samaritan in Your parable, may I too show mercy. Some may never enter the doors of a church, but what a difference an act of grace could make! Put before me opportunities to show unmerited favor. That is, after all, what You have shown to me. You died for my sins. I never could have earned salvation. It is a free gift, an act of grace. Make me merciful. Amen.

Which now of these three, thinkest thou, was neighbour unto him that fell among the thieves? And he said, He that shewed mercy on him. Then said Jesus unto him, Go, and do thou likewise.
LUKE 10:36–37 KJV

A Bold Faith

Because of what You've done, Jesus, my sins are forgiven and my transgressions are not counted against me. Through You, I am set apart. I have a hope and a future. I am considered righteous—but it's only through the glorious gift of God that I have a right standing with Him. And for this reason, I can live my life with confidence in You. I can stand solid in my faith, bold as a lion. Never let me take this precious gift for granted. Help me be brave, daring, and courageous even when people oppose Your truth. I will declare it and share it with others. Let my life be a testimony of Your great love.

|||||||||||||||||||||||||||||||||||||||||||||||||||||||||||||||||||||||||

A wicked person flees when no one is chasing him,
but righteous people are as bold as lions.
PROVERBS 28:1 GW

Our God Will Fight for Us

Heavenly Father, I totally depend on You always—but especially in the battle. Help me remember that I have a part as well. I will do all that is necessary to prepare for battle. My final confidence is in You, but I will not neglect doing what You tell me in Your Word. I will stand firm in faith. I will take up the full armor of God so that when the day of battle comes I am able to stand my ground. Then, having done everything I can, I will stand firm and watch You fight for me. You go before me. I am certain, with no doubt, that You will fight for me.

|||||||||||||||||||||||||||||||||||||||||||||||||||||||||||||||||||||||||||||

"When you hear the trumpet, assemble around me. Our God will fight for us!"
NEHEMIAH 4:20 GW

Loving Others

Father, sometimes it's hard for me to love the difficult people in my life. They feel like a daily chore I add to my to-do list and check off, and not like a growing relationship. Sometimes we don't agree on the same issue, or they make decisions that are drastically different from my own. I feel like they never listen to me or respect my feelings. Lord, there are days when I don't believe they deserve my love and forgiveness.

Help me to understand that my ability to love grows from Your love that I am firmly planted in. It shouldn't be about me or what I'm feeling. I know that You forgave my sins on the cross and loved me in my difficult moments. Since this is true, I am confident that I have the ability to love others when it's hard, because it's a reflection of the love You already poured onto me.

|||||||||||||||||||||||||||||||||||||||||||||||||||||||||||||||||||

We love because he first loved us.
1 JOHN 4:19 NIV

Joyful, Always!

Heavenly Father, I can be an emotional person. But even while acknowledging what is going on around me, I can still maintain my trust in You. I can be unshakable if I have established my dependence on You alone. I refuse to allow my circumstances to make me waver. I will remain cheerful no matter what because my joy comes from You. I will maintain an attitude of prayer, ready to receive from You. And I will live my life in Christ, fully unmovable in my decision to do what You say. As I do Your will, help me embrace a joyful and thankful way of thinking, always.

|||||||||||||||||||||||||||||||||||||||||||||||||||||||||||||||||||||||||

Be cheerful no matter what; pray all the time;
thank God no matter what happens. This is the
way God wants you who belong to Christ Jesus to live.
1 THESSALONIANS 5:16–18 MSG

22

Back Together Again

Lord, I've cried out to You in my troubles so many times, I've lost count. Thank You for always being there. No matter the number of times I fall apart, You always comfort me in the middle of grief, loss, sorrow, or failure. You are my promise, and I cling tightly to You. You hold me close and save me. Even though my tears blur my vision and I can't see where the pieces of my heart have been scattered, You pick up the fragments and put me back together again. You stand me up, strengthen me, and show me the truth of where I am, as only You can.

||||||||||||||||||||||||||||||||||||||||||||||||||||||||||||||||||||||||

The Lord is close to the brokenhearted and
saves those who are crushed in spirit.
PSALM 34:18 NIV

Invitation to Rest

Jesus, You told Your disciples to rest. You directed them to leave the crowd and to relax and eat. You saw that they had been busy with ministry and they needed to recuperate. If You directed them to rest, even these twelve who worked at Your side daily, You must want me to rest as well. Remind me to take breaks from ministry. I needed to hear that You give me permission to rest! Amen.

||||||||||||||||||||||||||||||||||||||||||||||||||||||||||||||||||||||

*And he said unto them, Come ye yourselves apart into a
desert place, and rest a while: for there were many coming
and going, and they had no leisure so much as to eat.*
MARK 6:31 KJV

When I Don't Want to Work

Lord, there are days when I find myself unmotivated and unwilling to do the work set before me. I am distracted by social media, burdened by circumstances, or uninterested in my current task. How can I find purpose in my jobs for today? How can I convince myself they matter?

Let me remember that I am ultimately working for You. When I focus on You and what You have asked me to do, I can be confident that my work matters. When I don't, I find myself avoiding my responsibilities and making moral compromises.

God, give me an overwhelming sense of duty and pride to know that I am performing for You. Help me return to work with renewed energy, focus, and purpose. The tasks I do and the way I work expand Your kingdom. Amen.

||||||||||||||||||||||||||||||||||||||||||||||||||||||||||||||||||||||||||

Whatever you do, work at it with all your heart,
as working for the Lord, not for human masters.
COLOSSIANS 3:23 NIV

Compassion

Jesus, I want to be filled with Your compassion. You love me unconditionally. Forgive me for thinking less of other people. No matter who they are or how different they are from me, You love them. And for that reason, I should show them Your love. Forgive me for being judgmental. Give me eyes of compassion to see them as You do. Give me opportunities to demonstrate kindness. Show me ways to bless those I would normally avoid. Remind me to pray for and acknowledge others just as You would.

|||||||||||||||||||||||||||||||||||||||||||||||||||||||||||||||||||||||||||||||||

Since you have been chosen by God who has given you this new kind of life, and because of his deep love and concern for you, you should practice tenderhearted mercy and kindness to others. Don't worry about making a good impression on them, but be ready to suffer quietly and patiently.
Colossians 3:12 tlb

Words Are Life

I can only image what it was like when You spoke the world into existence. Your words created the earth and everything in it. The sound of Your voice has indescribable power. My Bible is full of Your words. Through Your Word I have come to know You. Each chapter and verse is filled with wisdom and understanding for my life. It is food for my spirit. Help me remember when I read my Bible that Your Word gives me life. Your Word sustains me. And when I pray according to Your Word, all of heaven is backing me up. I rejoice in Your Word. As I go about my day, bring Your Word alive in me. Remind me of Your truth.

"Heaven and earth will pass away,
but my words will never pass away."
MATTHEW 24:35 NIV

First Place

I give Your Word first place in my life. I walk in the light of Your Word, stepping where You shine the light of truth, trusting that I am always in the right place at the right time in order to live according to Your purposes. In everything I do, I desire to bring You honor. I want to please You. I refuse to veer to the right or the left of the path You've set before me. It comforts me knowing You are always with me. I listen as Your voice speaks to me, telling me the way to go.

"So shall My word be that goes forth from My mouth; it shall not return to Me void, but it shall accomplish what I please, and it shall prosper in the thing for which I sent it."
ISAIAH 55:11 NKJV

A God-Centered Home

Father, so many homes are shaken in these days. So many families are shattering to pieces around me. Protect my home, I pray. Protect my loved ones. Be the foundation of my home, strong and solid, consistent and wise. May every decision made here reflect Your principles. May those who visit this home and encounter this family be keenly aware of our uniqueness, because we serve the one true and almighty God. Amen.

||||||||||||||||||||||||||||||||||||||||||||||||||||||||||||||||||||||||

Except the LORD build the house, they labour
in vain that build it: except the LORD keep the
city, the watchman waketh but in vain.
PSALM 127:1 KJV

Simply Follow

Forgive me, Lord, for making obedience harder than it is. I feel like I'm unprepared for what You've asked me to do, but really, I have a hard time letting go. Give me courage to step out, trusting You'll provide everything I need to accomplish the task. You will give me wisdom to act and the words to speak. You will equip me. All I have to do is follow You. I courageously declare that I will do what You've asked. I will step out in faith and trust You to meet me along the way.

||||||||||||||||||||||||||||||||||||||||||||||||||||||||||||||||||||||||||||||

The Spirit of the Sovereign LORD is on me, because the LORD has anointed me to proclaim good news to the poor. He has sent me to bind up the brokenhearted, to proclaim freedom for the captives and release from darkness for the prisoners.
ISAIAH 61:1 NIV

Restoration and Provision

Lord, my job is not my source. You are my source. You always provide for me. When my workplace is difficult, You help me be a blessing to others. When my employer is unfair, You are my justice. And if I lose my job, You will restore me to wealth. I will never go hungry or beg for bread. My needs are never a surprise to You; You know what I need before I ask You. And yet, I ask because You've asked me to do so. You abundantly supply my every need. It may be uncomfortable at times, but I will live by faith. I will stand firm and believe the best is yet to come.

|||||||||||||||||||||||||||||||||||||||||||||||||||||||||||||||||||||||||||||||

The Lord their God will take care of
them and will restore their fortunes.
ZEPHANIAH 2:7 GW

Unexpected Gifts

God, I am grateful for the surprises You bring into my life, even when they catch me unawares and I'm not quite sure how to respond. Everything that comes from You is good, so I must remember to look at Your unexpected acts as gifts from You. Help me keep an open mind when new things appear in my life suddenly. Help me pause and stay calm when it's not something I planned. Remind me to ask if this is a part of Your plan. Give me patience as the gifts You send unfold. Sometimes it takes a little time to see and understand the purpose You have in mind.

After all, he's famous for great and unexpected
acts; there's no end to his surprises.
JOB 5:9 MSG

Lord, I'm Tired

Lord, sometimes I feel like I don't have time to even breathe! My days are filled from the moment I wake up until the minute I go to bed. I tell myself I don't have time to rest because there is always one more thing to do, but You did not create Your children to live like this. On the seventh day of Creation, You rested. I can be positive that when I relax, I am not failing. I am preparing for the next task.

Teach me, God, to come to You when I'm tired and when I am overwhelmed. Only when I take the time to be in the presence of the Holy Spirit will I find myself truly refreshed, ready to take on what life has for me next. Help me to remember that You bring the greatest healing renewal.

||||||||||||||||||||||||||||||||||||||||||||||||||||||||||||||||||||||||||||||

"Come to me, all you who are weary
and burdened, and I will give you rest."
MATTHEW 11:28 NIV

Less Drama, More Peace

Lord, I come to You today asking for peace in my family. Thank You for Your Spirit living in us and with us. My family is blessed when we come in and when we go out with Your peace. No matter how much chaos is going on around us, we can rest and rely on You. Help us not to lose our composure when chaos erupts. Remind us to fix our minds and hearts on You. The world is filled with drama, but it doesn't have to be a part of our life. Help us keep Your peace as the center of our home.

||||||||||||||||||||||||||||||||||||||||||||||||||||||||||||||||||||||||||||

And all your [spiritual] children shall be disciples [taught by the Lord and obedient to His will], and great shall be the peace and undisturbed composure of your children.
ISAIAH 54:13 AMPC

My Keeper

Thank You, heavenly Father, for keeping me in all my ways. When I leave the house, I trust You to give me wisdom to navigate my day in safety so that I can return home without accident or incident. You give me strength when I am weary. You listen to my pleas for help as well as my praises. Your eyes are always on me, and Your ears are always listening for my voice. When I speak, You always hear me. You keep me steady. When I reach out to You, I find You. I can always depend on You. I am grateful for You, my Keeper!

||||||||||||||||||||||||||||||||||||||||||||||||||||||||||||||||||

He will guard and guide me, never letting me stumble or
fall. God is my keeper; he will never forget nor ignore me.
PSALM 121:3 TPT

God's Book of Wisdom

There are so many "how-to" books available today, Lord, and they all promise to increase my knowledge in some area. But not one of them gives any hope for added wisdom. Only Your Word offers that. Thank You for providing the means to know You more fully and to live life more abundantly. Amen.

||||||||||||||||||||||||||||||||||||||||||||||||||||||||||||||||||||||||

For the word of the LORD is right;
and all his works are done in truth.
PSALM 33:4 KJV

His Power at Work

Thank You, Lord, for the opportunity to live for You. I recognize the Holy Spirit's power at work in my life today. Just as I trusted Jesus to begin my new life by faith, I choose to live each day trusting Him. Guide me in all I do, as I submit to Your will. I desire to live my life in the flow of Your blessing. I seek to learn more each day as I grow in understanding and wisdom.

|||||||||||||||||||||||||||||||||||||||||||||||||||||||||||||||||||

In the same way you received Jesus our Lord and Messiah by faith, continue your journey of faith, progressing further into your union with him! Your spiritual roots go deeply into his life as you are continually infused with strength, encouraged in every way. For you are established in the faith you have absorbed and enriched by your devotion to him!
COLOSSIANS 2:6–7 TPT

Your Word Makes Anything Possible

Heavenly Father, Your Word is limitless and unbreakable. Thank You, God, for giving me Your Word—Your promises for all eternity. You cannot lie. You say it, and it is so. I choose to trust and believe Your Word above all else. I will grow in faith and stand firm on You and the power of Your Word. It is alive and working in my life. I know that when I speak Your truths and apply faith, the Word will accomplish what You send it to do in my life. You will keep me in perfect peace as I build my life on Your Word. Thank You for making the seemingly impossible a reality in my life.

|||||||||||||||||||||||||||||||||||||||||||||||||||||||||||||||||||||||||||

But Jesus looked at them and said to them, "With men this is impossible, but with God all things are possible."
MATTHEW 19:26 NKJV

To See the Victory

Lord, sometimes it's hard to see the victory hidden in life's circumstances. As You hung on the cross, Your followers perceived it as a crushing defeat. They couldn't see what You could see. Even as You assured them, they couldn't see how Your death could bring victory. But once You rose again, they learned the eternal joy of having You with them, always. Thank You for knowing the whole story. My victory is assured, and I will rejoice. I will see Your purpose and plan fulfilled in my life. You have made a way when I can't see it. So I put my trust in You today. Help me rest in You.

||||||||||||||||||||||||||||||||||||||||||||||||||||||||||||||||||||||||||||

"You have sorrow now, but I will see you again and then
you will rejoice; and no one can rob you of that joy."
JOHN 16:22 TLB

Dreams and Aspirations

Lord, I commit my aspirations to You. I believe that those dreams within my heart were placed there by You and that You have a plan to bring them to fruition. Give me the courage to work toward my goals and not be swayed by the opinions of others. Renew my mind and spirit so I'll be able to test and approve what Your will is—Your good, pleasing, and perfect will. Help me pace myself and learn the things I need to know before I put plans into motion. I will be humble and conscious of the hopes and hearts of others. I will praise You and give You all the glory as we work together for Your good.

|||||||||||||||||||||||||||||||||||||||||||||||||||||||||||||||||||||||||||||||||

The aspirations of good people end in celebration;
the ambitions of bad people crash.
PROVERBS 10:28 MSG

My Road, Revealed by God

Heavenly Father, I will stay true to You. You have placed me on the right path. Nothing can take me out of Your hand. I am confident in Your truth. You have plans for me, and those plans are good. You knew me before I was born, and You planned my way. You walk with me and talk with me. When I ask, You answer. When I look to the right or to the left, You whisper gently, "This is the way to go. Follow Me." I am focused. I will stay on course. I refuse to be deterred from walking the road You've chosen for me. Thank You that I don't ever have to walk alone.

|||||||||||||||||||||||||||||||||||||||||||||||||||||||||||||||||||||||||||

You're blessed when you stay on course,
walking steadily on the road revealed by GOD.
PSALM 119:1 MSG

Trust in His Guidance

Father, this morning I come before You and I praise You. You are good and loving. You have only my very best interests at heart. Take my hand and lead me. Show me the way to go. Like a child being carried in a loving parent's arms, let me relax and trust You. I know that You will never lead me astray. Thank You, God, for this assurance. Amen.

|||||||||||||||||||||||||||||||||||||||||||||||||||||||||||||||||||||||||||||

Cause me to hear thy lovingkindness in the morning;
for in thee do I trust: cause me to know the way wherein
I should walk; for I lift up my soul unto thee.
PSALM 143:8 KJV

Navigating Decisions

Lord, I desire to please You more than anything else. Help me ask You the right questions in order to sense Your wisdom and realize the answers You have for me. Help me not to be afraid of the answers but to trust You. Please show me how You look at this situation. Give me eyes to see things from the right perspective. Help me learn and grow in my faith as I navigate this decision. Help me let go of any thoughts that are contrary to Your Word. I trust You will give me the answers I need so I understand clearly the next step to take.

||||||||||||||||||||||||||||||||||||||||||||||||||||||||||||||||||||||||||

But let endurance and steadfastness and patience
have full play and do a thorough work, so that
you may be [people] perfectly and fully developed
[with no defects], lacking in nothing.
JAMES 1:4 AMPC

Give Hope. Give Life.

Mighty God, You are my hope. You have given me life and delivered me from death. My faith is rising. I believe I will receive all that You have prepared for me. My life is Yours to command. I look to You for all the answers. When I don't yet see what You see, help my unbelief. Holy Spirit, please let me see what You see, and make me courageous enough to follow through with Your divine appointments—encounters that could change a life. I trust You. I know You are my reward. I earnestly seek to know You more.

But without faith it is impossible to please and be satisfactory to Him. For whoever would come near to God must [necessarily] believe that God exists and that He is the rewarder of those who earnestly and diligently seek Him [out].
HEBREWS 11:6 AMPC

Daily Guidance

Forgive me, Father, for the times I've run to You only when life gets difficult. I know I should seek Your guidance by being in Your presence every day. Help me say no to distractions that would keep me from spending time with You. Fill me with an overwhelming desire to be with You. Help me continually seek You so that I am always prepared for any challenge of life. Through Your daily guidance I can better navigate the obstacles in life and in many cases avoid them. Draw me to You, God. May I hunger and thirst after You!

||||||||||||||||||||||||||||||||||||||||||||||||||||||||||||||||||||||

Hear my cry. Show me mercy, and send the
help I need! I heard your voice in my heart say,
"Come, seek my face," my inner being responded,
"Yahweh, I'm seeking your face with all my heart."
PSALM 27:7–8 TPT

My Hope Rises

Jesus, Your words in the Bible encourage me. I speak Your Word with my mouth, and hope rises in my heart. I will fight fear with faith knowing Your glory and truth will overcome the darkness. No darkness can withstand even a sliver of light. I choose to walk in Your light each day. Your gift of resurrection life pushes back the darkness. When I am tempted to allow the darkness to creep into my thoughts, remind me to shine Your light on those thoughts, knowing it will expel the darkness.

Arise, shine; for your light has come! And the glory of the Lord is risen upon you. For behold, the darkness shall cover the earth, and deep darkness the people; but the Lord will arise over you, and His glory will be seen upon you.
Isaiah 60:1–2 nkjv

Praying for Bold Faith

I desire a bold faith, Jesus. Like the woman who followed You, crying out, asking that You cast a demon from her daughter. She was a Gentile, not a Jew; yet she called You the "Son of David." She acknowledged You as the Messiah. And You stopped. Her faith impressed You. You healed the child. May I be so bold. May I recognize that You are the only solution to every problem. Amen.

||||||||||||||||||||||||||||||||||||||||||||||||||||||||||||||||||||||

Then Jesus answered and said unto her, O woman,
great is thy faith: be it unto thee even as thou wilt.
And her daughter was made whole from that very hour.
MATTHEW 15:28 KJV

You Do Miracles

Thank You for doing miracles in my heart and in my life. Forgive me when I've doubted, and help me trust You more each day. When You speak to me and give me a promise, I will hold fast to it. I will believe You and encourage myself in Your Word. Even when the miracle looks like the smallest thing—such as a cloud the size of a man's fist—I will stand strong and see the rain poured out lavishly on my life. Your Word says we all have a measure of faith given to us. I will use my faith today to believe that You will faithfully complete the work You've begun in me.

‖‖‖

You are the God who performs miracles. You have made your strength known among the nations.
PSALM 77:14 GW

48

When I Worry

Father, sometimes I don't come to You with all my problems. I'm afraid that my everyday struggles may be insignificant compared to other things happening in the world. I try to deal with them on my own or seek out other comforts. These sometimes don't solve the issue, or they can solve the problem but leave me feeling exhausted.

Thank You, Lord, for reminding me that You care about the details of our lives. You ask us to come to You with every burden, big or small. When we cast our anxieties on You, we can find answers to our problems and peace to our hearts. Today I give all my worries to You. I choose to believe You care deeply and will do what is best for me and the ones I love. I will not focus anymore on the things I ask You to control.

|||||||||||||||||||||||||||||||||||||||||||||||||||||||||||||||||||||||

Cast all your anxiety on him because he cares for you.
1 PETER 5:7 NIV

Teach Me to Pray

When I pray, I grow in faith. In Your presence my doubts and fears die. In Your presence my ability to trust You grows. Like Jesus, I want to be rooted in prayer. I want to walk in Your power and authority with signs and wonders. Just as Jesus taught His disciples to pray, I ask You, God, to teach me to pray. Help me to make prayer a priority, to esteem my time with You and guard it as a precious opportunity. May You find me daily on my knees before You, where I receive the strength and the courage I need to face the challenges of this fallen world.

Once Jesus was praying in a certain place. When he stopped praying, one of his disciples said to him, "Lord, teach us to pray as John taught his disciples."
LUKE 11:1 GW

Set for Life

God, my life is in You. You alone are my rest. I find peace in Your presence. Thank You for Your all-surpassing strength. When I stumble, You hold me up. I refuse to be shaken by the challenges facing me. When I can't catch my breath, You pour oxygen into my soul. I will not be moved when things don't go my way. I will rise above the disappointment because my future is assured. Because of You, I am set for life. In You, I have everything I need.

||||||||||||||||||||||||||||||||||||||||||||||||||||||||||||||||||||||||

God, the one and only—I'll wait as long as he says.
Everything I hope for comes from him, so why not?
He's solid rock under my feet, breathing room for
my soul, an impregnable castle: I'm set for life.
PSALM 62:5–6 MSG

Come to Jesus

I come to You, Lord Jesus. That is the first step. I come before You now in this quiet moment. As I begin this new day, calm my spirit. There is work that must be done today. But even as I work, I can find rest in You. Ease the tension and stress in me, Lord, as only You can do. Thank You for a sense of peace. Amen.

||||||||||||||||||||||||||||||||||||||||||||||||||||||||||||||||||||||

*Come unto me, all ye that labour and are
heavy laden, and I will give you rest.*
MATTHEW 11:28 KJV

To Speak the Truth, Always

Lord, let the words of my mouth and the meditations of my heart be pleasing in Your sight. Your Word says that life and death are in the power of my tongue. I know what is in my heart comes out of my mouth. Help me pause and think before I speak, especially in delicate or awkward situations. Create in me a clean heart. Holy Spirit, fill me with a new attitude and new motives. Quicken my heart to hear things the way You do. Tune my ear to hear what I'm saying. Help me speak with love and kindness.

|||||||||||||||||||||||||||||||||||||||||||||||||||||||||||||||||||||||||

"Your very words will be used as evidence, and your words will declare you either innocent or guilty."
MATTHEW 12:37 TPT

Restore, Heal, and Cure

God, You are my Creator. You know me from the inside out. When You created me, You made me individual and unique. Every challenge I've had with my health is no mystery to You. Doctors may treat an ailment, but You restore me, heal me, and cure me. You deliver me body, mind, and spirit. You know my emotional state and what things impact me positively and negatively. You will never give up on me. You will never fail me. Thank You for being there every single time I need You. Reach into me and bring about life-giving health as only You can.

"As for you, I'll come with healing, curing the incurable, because they all gave up on you and dismissed you as hopeless—that good-for-nothing Zion."
JEREMIAH 30:17 MSG

Run to God!

Father, on hard days, help me not to grumble or fuss with You like a small child. Shut my mouth so I don't complain to others. I can be such a whiner! When I am angry, teach me to run *to* You instead of *away* from You. When I encounter difficulty or disappointment, remind me that I can never hide from You. When I feel scared, weak, or alone, hold me tight and don't let me go. Lift my heart and give me strength. Remind me of all You've done. Bring Your promises to life in me, and help me push through the hard places. I do love You with all my heart and soul. You are my strength in every circumstance—good or bad.

||||||||||||||||||||||||||||||||||||||||||||||||||||||||||||||||||||||||

The Lord is a strong fortress.
The godly run to him and are safe.
PROVERBS 18:10 TLB

Whispers of Encouragement

Lord, You've given me all the answers. They are found in Your Word. When I feel lost and far from You, please remind me of Your truth. Let Your words speak to me as though You were whispering encouragement and direction into my ear. Hold me up with the power of Your Word when I feel defeated. Give me strength when I feel drained by my circumstances. Direct my eyes to the scriptures You would have me read for the answers I need today. You know what I need before I even ask.

||||||||||||||||||||||||||||||||||||||||||||||||||||||||||||||||||||||

"This Book of the Law shall not depart from your mouth,
but you shall meditate in it day and night, that you
may observe to do according to all that is written
in it. For then you will make your way prosperous,
and then you will have good success."
JOSHUA 1:8 NKJV

Following
Christ's Example

Lord, You are always there, and You are consistently patient with me. What if it were not so? What if You reached Your limit and showed the wrath that I deserve in my sinful imperfection? Because of Your great patience with me, let me not grow tired of being patient myself. Let me model what You have shown me by Your example. Thank You for Your great patience with me, God. Amen.

|||||||||||||||||||||||||||||||||||||||||||||||||||||||||||||||||||||||||

And let us not be weary in well doing: for in due season we shall reap, if we faint not.
GALATIANS 6:9 KJV

Right Words

God, I need Your help. I need a lot of courage for a difficult conversation I must have. I have to tell someone something that's tough to say. I need to be truthful, but it's so hard, God. Please give me the right words. Help me say things in a way that will help and not hurt. Please speak through me. Prepare her heart for what You would have me say. Give me Your grace to do what is necessary.

|||||||||||||||||||||||||||||||||||||||||||||||||||||||||||||||||||||||

We should no longer be children, tossed to and fro
and carried about with every wind of doctrine, by the
trickery of men, in the cunning craftiness of deceitful
plotting, but, speaking the truth in love, may grow
up in all things into Him who is the head—Christ.
EPHESIANS 4:14–15 NKJV

Overflowing Life

God, You are the giver of life. You hold my times in Your hands. But You've also enriched my life in ways I've never dreamed. You fill me to overflowing. Help me to always be watchful and aware of the enemy's plans. I will not be fearful of him but rely on You to keep me in all my ways. I am wise and have great understanding and discernment from You so that I stay on Your path. I will keep my eyes on You. I am laser focused. Thank You for every blessing. Even in the challenging times, You teach me Your ways and fill me with Your love.

|||||||||||||||||||||||||||||||||||||||||||||||||||||||||||||||||||||||

The thief comes only in order to steal and kill and destroy. I came that they may have and enjoy life, and have it in abundance (to the full, till it overflows).
JOHN 10:10 AMPC

To Answer the Call

Thank You, Lord, for knocking on the door of my heart. Thank You for giving me the courage to answer and invite You into my life. Now I ask You to help me encourage others to answer that same knock on their heart's door. Help me pay attention when You bring people across my path who are ready for a seed of hope to be planted in their hearts. Give me Your words to speak into their lives; guide me in actions that support them. May I respond with a heart of compassion and a disciplined life as an example to them.

Behold, I stand at the door and knock; if anyone hears and listens to and heeds My voice and opens the door, I will come in to him and will eat with him, and he [will eat] with Me.
REVELATION 3:20 AMPC

Being Mean

In times of stress, I find myself snapping at the people around me. I can be mean and say hurtful things to my friends, family, and coworkers. This comes from my desire to be right, my own pride, and my fear of being intimidated. Father, every day I have to be reminded to love the way Jesus does—with nothing asked in return, to care even when it's hard.

In the end, Jesus did the same for me. Instead of accusing me and leaving me in my sin, He chose to bear it all. He sacrificed Himself not only for me but for all His children. I have no right to treat people any less than that. Help me to be kind and to forgive others when I feel wronged. Teach me to speak out of the love You have shown me instead of lashing out.

||||||||||||||||||||||||||||||||||||||||||||||||||||||||||||||||||||||||||||

Be kind and compassionate to one another,
forgiving each other, just as in Christ God forgave you.
EPHESIANS 4:32 NIV

Unswerving Love

From the beginning of time, You had a plan for me. You loved me so much, You refused to lose. You sacrificed for the opportunity of a relationship with me. Oh, how great is Your unswerving love. You will never give up on me, no matter how many times I fail, no matter how many times I come to You asking for forgiveness. Thank You for Your great mercy. Thank You for guiding me with Your steady hand. May I always see Your love at every turn of the path You've set before me. I am no longer of this world but forever belong to You. May I live each day fully aware of Your sacrificial love for me.

But God showed his great love for us by sending Christ to die for us while we were still sinners.
ROMANS 5:8 TLB

Rescue Me

"Lord, listen to my prayer. It's like a sacrifice I bring to you; I must have more revelation of your Word! Take my words to heart when I ask you, Lord; rescue me, just like you promised! I offer you my joyous praise for all that you've taught me. Your wonderful words will become my song of worship, for everything you've commanded is perfect and true. Place your hands of strength and favor upon me, for I've made my choice to follow your ways. I wait for your deliverance, O Lord, for your words thrill me like nothing else! Invigorate my life so that I can praise you even more, and may your truth be my strength!" (Psalm 119:169–175 TPT).

|||||||||||||||||||||||||||||||||||||||||||||||||||||||||||||||||||||||||

I'll never forget what you've taught me, Lord,
but when I wander off and lose my way,
come after me, for I am your beloved!
PSALM 119:176 TPT

Prioritizing

Father, I really have a lot to do, and I'm not very good at multi-tasking. I need Your help each day as I organize the chores that need to be done. Show me how to prioritize my workload so that I can get things done in the most efficient manner, and let my work be pleasing in Your sight. Amen.

||||||||||||||||||||||||||||||||||||||||||||||||||||||||||||||||||||||||

But seek ye first the kingdom of God, and his righteousness;
and all these things shall be added unto you.
MATTHEW 6:33 KJV

My Place in Prayer

Lord, I am a part of the household of faith. My connection to the family of God defines who I am. I am confident of my spiritual heritage and my eternal home in heaven. I am committed to prayer. It is the way I communicate with You. Through prayer our relationship grows. Through daily meditation I better understand myself and the heart of the Father. I grow in my trust and discover His will and His purposes. Thank You for my place in prayer. May I remain committed to my quiet moments with You. May our times together nurture my faith.

But Christ is a faithful son in charge of God's household.
We are his household if we continue to have courage
and to be proud of the confidence we have.
HEBREWS 3:6 GW

Holding on to Hope

Lord, I refuse to quit! I'm holding on to hope. My hope is in You, my rock and my Redeemer. If I did quit, I realize I would just become stuck. The only way out is to put one foot in front of the other. Give me strength to endure this season. Eventually it will pass. I must keep pressing on day after day. I will come out of this on the other side. I will look back and see just how far we've come together. I wait with expectation, even if the end is not in sight. I won't let go. You are the answer. You are where I've placed my hope.

|||||||||||||||||||||||||||||||||||||||||||||||||||||||||||||||||||||||

Wait, Israel, for GOD. Wait with hope.
Hope now; hope always!
PSALM 131:3 MSG

Powerful Words

Father, Your Word is life to me. It brings me peace, security, joy, and understanding about who You are and who You've created me to be. Help me be a student of Your Word. I put Your Word in my heart so that it is with me when I need it most. I speak Your truth and it silences the words of doubt and fear that Satan whispers to bring worry and anxiety into my life. May Your life-giving words always triumph over any other voice I hear.

||||||||||||||||||||||||||||||||||||||||||||||||||||||||||||||||||||||||

*Dear friend, listen well to my words; tune your
ears to my voice. Keep my message in plain
view at all times. Concentrate! Learn it by heart!
Those who discover these words live, really live;
body and soul, they're bursting with health.*
PROVERBS 4:20–22 MSG

Truth's Shining Light

Heavenly Father, thank You for the Bible. It is filled with everything I need to follow after You. Like a bright flashlight in the darkest of nights, it shows me the way forward toward the life You have for me. It guides me in wisdom, helping me see the stumbling blocks in my way so that I can navigate carefully over them without falling. When I am frustrated or confused, Your truth makes the way clear for me. When my heart is troubled about life's circumstances, Your words bring me back to a place of peace found only in You.

Truth's shining light guides me in my choices and decisions;
the revelation of your Word makes my pathway clear.
PSALM 119:105 TPT

Appreciate the Moment

God, the world is moving so fast! I think about all the changes I've seen in my lifetime, and it's amazing. Sometimes I just want to make time stand still. Today, I stand still and drink in Your peace. I recall the times of Your goodness. I look at the life You've given me, and I listen. I take in the minutes and seconds. I appreciate this moment in time. Help me not to lose sight of You in the blur of my days. I loosen my grip and let go of all of life's pressures. I relish this quiet time and relax in Your presence.

|||||||||||||||||||||||||||||||||||||||||||||||||||||||||||||||||||||||

Let be and be still, and know (recognize and understand) that I am God. I will be exalted among the nations! I will be exalted in the earth!
PSALM 46:10 AMPC

Fear No Evil

How wonderful, God, that death has no power over the Christian! You are a strong and mighty God, the one true God. You are with me, protecting me all the way. And when the end of this life comes, whenever that may be, You will walk with me through the valley of the shadow of death. Death has lost its sting because Christ has conquered it! In Your name I pray, amen.

Yea, though I walk through the valley of the shadow of death, I will fear no evil: for thou art with me; thy rod and thy staff they comfort me.
PSALM 23:4 KJV

Placing Worry in His Hands

Father, strengthen my heart. Give me the courage I need to overcome fear. I know that You love me and watch over my family and friends far better than I can. I come to You with palms up and arms open wide. I release what I want to hold close. I give You the lives of those I love. I can't protect them or make their lives better. Help me put my worries about them in Your hands. You know their names. You love them more than I do. Give me peace as I let go of them today.

||||||||||||||||||||||||||||||||||||||||||||||||||||||||||||||||||||

"Who will not fear you, Lord, and bring glory to your name?
For you alone are holy. All nations will come and worship
before you, for your righteous acts have been revealed."
REVELATION 15:4 NIV

Miracles Every Day

Lord, You are the miracle maker. Forgive me when I miss the small, everyday miracles. Help me see everything You are doing, all that You provide in my life. Teach me to be grateful for every gift You give. I will rejoice for every breath I take and every provision You make. I know You do great things. I believe You can bring the dead back to life. You make a way when there seems to be no way. You keep me from harm. I celebrate You, Lord! Thank You for being at work in my life even now, in this very moment.

|||||||||||||||||||||||||||||||||||||||||||||||||||||||||||||||||||||||||||||||

Jesus turned around and, seeing her, He said,
Take courage, daughter! Your faith has made you well.
And at once the woman was restored to health.
MATTHEW 9:22 AMPC

No One Loves
Me Like You Do

Lord, You have always known everything there is to know about me. You realize every movement of my heart and soul, and You comprehend every thought before it ever enters my mind. My heart is Your open book, and You know all the words I'll say in a day before my feet hit the ground. You know every step I will take before my journey even begins. You've gone into my future to prepare my way. Thank You for Your hand of love on my life and for the blessings You impart to me. There is no one who loves me like You do.

||||||||||||||||||||||||||||||||||||||||||||||||||||||||||||||||||||

You saw who you created me to be before I became me!
Before I'd ever seen the light of day, the number of days
you planned for me were already recorded in your book.
PSALM 139:16 TPT

Committed to the Journey

God, I want to continue to grow. Let my words, my thoughts, and my choices be pleasing to You. May all that I do be a witness to others. Sometimes it's hard to step out in faith because I don't know all the details. I must trust that You have a good reason for asking me to do this next thing. The secret to change in my life is to give all to You—to let go and let You work everything out for my good. Help me stay committed to the journey ahead, and remind me that others are watching.

|||||||||||||||||||||||||||||||||||||||||||||||||||||||||||||||||||||||||||||

*If I am being poured out as a drink offering on the sacrifice
and service of your faith, I am glad and rejoice with you all.
For the same reason you also be glad and rejoice with me.*
PHILIPPIANS 2:17–18 NKJV

My Source of Strength

Father, at times I worry too much about what others think of me. Even when I just have a minor disagreement with a friend or coworker, I am afraid that the person will not like me anymore. I worry that I have not lived up to what was expected of me. Remind me, Father, that I must seek my ultimate strength and encouragement from You and You alone. Amen.

||||||||||||||||||||||||||||||||||||||||||||||||||||||||||||||||||||||

And David was greatly distressed; for the people spake of stoning him, because the soul of all the people was grieved, every man for his sons and for his daughters: but David encouraged himself in the Lord his God.
1 SAMUEL 30:6 KJV

Help Me Hope Again

Lord, You make all things beautiful in their time. My life looks so different today from how it looked before I met You. I know You are working on me. Sometimes it's hard to escape the pain. Tears cloud my vision, and I struggle to find my way. But I know You are making me new. I won't give up hope because Your promises are true. Even though I can't see it now, You have a plan to use me in wonderful ways. I give my all to You. Mold me, shape me. Help me hope again.

|||||||||||||||||||||||||||||||||||||||||||||||||||||||||||||||||||||||||

He has made everything beautiful in its time. Also He has put eternity in their hearts, except that no one can find out the work that God does from beginning to end.
ECCLESIASTES 3:11 NKJV

Fight My Battles

Father, You've told me who the enemy is. I'm not fighting with men and women. But we are fighting powers we cannot see. Remind me not to blame people when they are used by the enemy. I will keep my focus on You. You fight my battles for me. Give me a courageous heart so I can fight this fight with faith. I praise You in the middle of the battle. You have already declared me victorious. I am guaranteed a win—as long as I stand on Your side, the side of truth!

|||||||||||||||||||||||||||||||||||||||||||||||||||||||||||||||||||||||||

For we do not wrestle against flesh and blood,
but against principalities, against powers,
against the rulers of the darkness of this age, against
spiritual hosts of wickedness in the heavenly places.
EPHESIANS 6:12 NKJV

Holy Spirit Power

Lord, today I pray for my family. As we go through this life, we each are tempted at times. I stand firm in faith that we will not falter. The Holy Spirit goes with my family, giving them the power to stand against any temptation. Holy Spirit, remind them who they are in Christ. Give them the Word of God to speak in the face of the enemy. May they always choose truth and life. Let them not be deceived in any way. May they hear the voice of wisdom saying, "This is the way, walk in it." Infuse them with strength and power today.

|||||||||||||||||||||||||||||||||||||||||||||||||||||||||||||||||||||||||||||||

Jesus, full of the Holy Spirit, left the Jordan River, being urged by the Spirit out into the barren wastelands of Judea, where Satan tempted him for forty days.

LUKE 4:1–2 TLB

Fear Can Never Conquer Me

God, Your Word says that You have given me a spirit of power, of love, and of a sound mind instead of fear. No matter how hard the season or how dark the night, fear has no place in my life. It will not conquer me because You defeated fear for me. I stay close to You, always in Your presence. You are my strength and my peace. Your comfort surrounds me. Your perfect love casts away all fear.

||||||||||||||||||||||||||||||||||||||||||||||||||||||||||||||||||||||||||

*Even when your path takes me through the valley
of deepest darkness, fear will never conquer me,
for you already have! Your authority is my strength
and my peace. The comfort of your love takes away
my fear. I'll never be lonely, for you are near.*
PSALM 23:4 TPT

Say and Do Good

Lord, my words really matter. What I say about myself and about others is important. My words lead to actions, and my actions demonstrate the fruit growing in my life. I want to please You and produce good fruit for others to see—the kind of fruit that points them to You. Please place a guard over my mouth. Help me think about the words I say before I speak them. I want my words and actions to bring blessing and life into my life and into the lives of others. May I be an encourager who offers hope in all I say and do.

|||||||||||||||||||||||||||||||||||||||||||||||||||||||||||||||||||||||||||

God our Father loved us and by his kindness gave us everlasting encouragement and good hope. Together with our Lord Jesus Christ, may he encourage and strengthen you to do and say everything that is good.
2 THESSALONIANS 2:16–17 GW

Stomp out the Doubt

When I am tempted to doubt the promises You've made, I will grow my expectations. I will dream big. I take my what-ifs and why-nots and I stomp them to the ground. Doubt and unbelief are not thoughts from You. Your Word says the devil is under my feet. So I place those thoughts that are against Your truth under my feet too. I remember Your Word. I will be brave and courageous. I will not give up. I will hold tightly to hope; hope is my anchor. I will endure. I will not be defeated. All of Your promises are yes and amen.

Wait and hope for and expect the Lord; be brave and of good courage and let your heart be stout and enduring. Yes, wait for and hope for and expect the Lord.
PSALM 27:14 AMPC

Wise Counsel

Lord, I've been praying a long time about this situation, but it never seems to change. I'm asking You now, what should I do? Is it time for a different plan? Lead me to people who aren't afraid to speak truth into my life. Prepare their hearts to speak by Your Holy Spirit. Bring truth and wise counsel. Through their lives, their words, and their love for me, allow me to see what I might be missing. Once they've spoken Your truth, confirm it in Your Word. Let me know through scripture and revelation that You are leading me.

||||||||||||||||||||||||||||||||||||||||||||||||||||||||||||||||||||||

*Where no wise guidance is, the people fall, but in
the multitude of counselors there is safety.*
PROVERBS 11:14 AMPC

A Load of Stress

Deadlines, sports schedules, unexpected overnight company—I'm about to pull out my hair! I know we all have our share of stress, but didn't I get an extra load this week, Father? I'm not sure what the purpose of it is, but I know there's a reason. Lord, give me patience through the ordeal, and let me please You. Amen.

||||||||||||||||||||||||||||||||||||||||||||||||||||||||||||||||||

*Take my yoke upon you, and learn of me; for I am meek
and lowly in heart: and ye shall find rest unto your
souls. For my yoke is easy, and my burden is light.*
MATTHEW 11:29–30 KJV

I Know You Love Me

I trust You, Lord. I am learning every day that no one else could ever love me like You do. I look at true human love in my life, and I realize Your love is beyond measure. No matter what comes my way, nothing can remove me from Your hand. Your unconditional, all-consuming love is powerful. It gives me the strength I need to step out in faith, to believe what others perceive as unbelievable. You counted me worthy of Your love, so I know I am precious and valuable.

||||||||||||||||||||||||||||||||||||||||||||||||||||||||||||||||||||||

For I am persuaded that neither death nor life,
nor angels nor principalities nor powers, nor things
present nor things to come, nor height nor depth,
nor any other created thing, shall be able to separate us
from the love of God which is in Christ Jesus our Lord.
ROMANS 8:38–39 NKJV

Going to God for Guilt

When I feel guilty, my first instinct is to hide from You, Lord. I forget that You know everything about me and love me anyway. You ask me to come to You for repentance and love while the enemy wants me to stay in darkness.

The fear to approach You in my times of guilt is from my own want to be perfect. If I rely on this way of thinking, it could lead to even more heartache.

God, it is hard for me to accept that coming to You in my need and hurt is a sign of weakness. But my strength comes from only You and not from me. While I try to fix my feelings on my own, You offer acceptance and forgiveness. I will rest in that truth today. I am forgiven!

||||||||||||||||||||||||||||||||||||||||||||||||||||||||||||||||||||||||||

Godly sorrow brings repentance that leads to salvation
and leaves no regret, but worldly sorrow brings death.
2 CORINTHIANS 7:10 NIV

Pursue the New

Thank You for my new life. I am reborn in Christ, but sometimes I slip back into my old thought patterns, remembering who I was before. I know I should not beat myself up about my past. I am not that old person. I have a new life, new hopes, new dreams. As I study Your Word, help me renew my mind with the truth of who I am now and who You have created me to be. I intentionally put my past behind me. I focus on my future in You. Give me grace to forgive myself, to look past my failures, and to humbly pursue the new.

||||||||||||||||||||||||||||||||||||||||||||||||||||||||||||||||||||||

*Anyone united with the Messiah gets a fresh start,
is created new. The old life is gone; a new life emerges!*
2 CORINTHIANS 5:17 MSG

A New Thing

New seasons can be exciting, but they're not without challenges.
I want to be excited about what You are going to do. I will not
camp out on past failures or things I wish could have stayed the
same. You have a purpose to every season. I am waiting and
watching. I am expecting the new. I believe it will be a glorious
surprise. I will not cower in trepidation but instead embrace it
with joy. Give me excitement for this new thing.

||||||||||||||||||||||||||||||||||||||||||||||||||||||||||||||||||

*Do not [earnestly] remember the former things;
neither consider the things of old. Behold, I am doing
a new thing! Now it springs forth; do you not perceive
and know it and will you not give heed to it? I will even
make a way in the wilderness and rivers in the desert.*
ISAIAH 43:18–19 AMPC

Humility of Heart

I've worked hard, Lord. I've prayed, believed, and expected. I've imagined how You would promote me and bring blessing to my life. But I am learning that my way is not the way You will do it. Knocking down doors and placing myself above others, even if I think I deserve it, is not Your way. Forgive me for trying to make things happen. I want to do things the right way—Your way. I humble myself before You. I acknowledge that whatever happens for my good is not about me but about You at work *in* me. It is Your favor at work. Give me patience to wait for Your timing and the right promotion.

||||||||||||||||||||||||||||||||||||||||||||||||||||||||||||||||||||||||||||

Humble yourselves in the Lord's presence.
Then he will give you a high position.
JAMES 4:10 GW

God Knows Me

God, the Bible says that You knew me even before I was formed in my mother's womb. I find confidence in this. You have been with me all along this journey! As I face this day, help me to remember that I am never alone. You go before me to prepare the future. You walk with me through the present. And You were there with me since before I was born. Wow! Amen.

||||||||||||||||||||||||||||||||||||||||||||||||||||||||||||||||||||

*For thou hast possessed my reins: thou hast covered
me in my mother's womb. I will praise thee; for I am
fearfully and wonderfully made: marvellous are thy
works; and that my soul knoweth right well.*

PSALM 139:13–14 KJV

Refuse to Quit

Lord, sometimes I want to say, "Beam me up, God!" I want to escape this place, with all its troubles and temptations. But You have given me life and definite purpose. I know You have work for me to do here. You know my passion. You created me with a uniqueness. I can do something no one else can do. I can touch lives perhaps no one else can touch for You. Let me help the hungry, the oppressed, the imprisoned, the homeless, and the wounded. Show me the plans You have for me. Give me strength for today. I refuse to quit! I will do all that You've asked me to do.

*"But take courage, O Zerubbabel and Joshua
and all the people; take courage and work,
for I am with you, says the Lord Almighty."*
HAGGAI 2:4 TLB

God Thoughts

God, sometimes negative thoughts consume me. I want to think Your thoughts for me, for my life, and for my future. I want to take my negative thoughts and turn them around so that they become positive, faith-filled affirmations. I will pay more attention to what I'm thinking. I choose to think on the truth, the reputable, honorable things. I need Your help keeping those negative, tempting, and worrisome thoughts under control. So I give You authority in my life to help me deal with my thoughts. Help me keep my mind on You.

|||||||||||||||||||||||||||||||||||||||||||||||||||||||||||||||||||||||

Finally, brethren, whatever things are true, whatever things are noble, whatever things are just, whatever things are pure, whatever things are lovely, whatever things are of good report, if there is any virtue and if there is anything praiseworthy—meditate on these things.
PHILIPPIANS 4:8 NKJV

My Help Comes from the Lord

Heavenly Father, I come to You first. I will overcome this world, just as Jesus did, through prayer. Help me remember that I don't have to do this life alone. You are with me—helping me, guiding me, protecting me, and cheering me on. I receive strength from You. I listen to Your wisdom. As I spend time with You, I emerge confident and strong. I hold fast to You knowing the storms of life will not take me out. Whatever I need today, You will provide it. I refuse to lose. I will not give up. Keep me in all my ways as I acknowledge You today.

‖‖

Shall I look to the mountain gods for help?
No! My help is from Jehovah who made
the mountains! And the heavens too!
PSALM 121:1–2 TLB

A Place of Peace

Lord, You are my peace. I can't find peace in anyone or anything else. This world is full of chaos, and it does its best to crowd into my space. But You are my rock, my confidence. I can step away from the race happening in this world. I can sit down in the quiet of Your presence and experience great peace—Your peace, not my own. Surround me even now, like a cloud, and go before me. Embrace me in Your peace that I may carry it with me and share it with others.

|||||||||||||||||||||||||||||||||||||||||||||||||||||||||||||||||||||||||||||

Until at last the Spirit is poured down on us from heaven. Then once again enormous crops will come. Then justice will rule through all the land, and out of justice, peace. Quietness and confidence will reign forever more.
Isaiah 32:15–17 TLB

God Hears My Prayers

Lord, the gods of other religions are not approachable. Their subjects bow before them in anguish, hoping to find favor in their sight. These gods are not real. You are the one true and living God, a loving heavenly Father. I love that Your Word says I can come before You with confidence. You hear my prayers. You know my heart. Thank You, Father. Speak to my heart as I meditate upon Your Word now. Amen.

And this is the confidence that we have in him, that, if we ask any thing according to his will, he heareth us.
1 John 5:14 kjv

Committed to Your Word

I love Your Word. Your ways are always just and right. I take the path You have chosen for me because Your Word preserves my life. I will walk in the way Your Word compels me to go. Help me follow hard after You with all my heart. Help me keep my heart right so that I always do what pleases You most. When I am weary, help me keep Your commandments. When I am not sure which way to go, light my way with biblical truths. I am committed to Your Word, God. I take it to heart so that I will not sin against You. Help me hear Your voice directing my path!

||||||||||||||||||||||||||||||||||||||||||||||||||||||||||||||||||||||||||

How I long for your precepts! In your
righteousness preserve my life.
PSALM 119:40 NIV

Courage to Forgive

Jesus, You always forgive. You show compassion and are slow to anger. I know that's also the way I should be. When people hurt me, remind me to love like You do. Give me the courage to forgive even while they are doing what hurts me. As those who crucified You were nailing You to the cross, You prayed for the Father to forgive them. You had compassion, saying they didn't know what they were doing. Let my heart be filled with compassion for those who have hurt me or hurt someone I love. Let me truly let it go today. Fill my heart with understanding of just how much You love them. Let me see them like You do.

The soldiers, after they crucified him,
gambled over his clothing.
LUKE 23:34 TPT

Live an Authentic Life

It takes courage to live in Your light. It takes courage to remove the mask and live genuinely. I've watched the hypocrite and pretender. At times, I've even been one. But I am no longer a daughter of the dark; in Christ I am a child of the light. I can live with nothing to hide—no sin, no hypocrisy, no pretensions, nothing. I choose today to embrace the real me. I owe it to You, God, and to myself to live an authentic life.

You groped your way through that murk once, but no longer. You're out in the open now. The bright light of Christ makes your way plain. So no more stumbling around. Get on with it! The good, the right, the true— these are the actions appropriate for daylight hours.

EPHESIANS 5:8–9 MSG

Face-to-Face

I am created for relationship with You. Remind me daily that You desire face time with me. Just as You walked in the garden with Adam and talked with him, You desire that same fellowship with me. I will take time for You. I will not allow the busyness of life to overcrowd us. Help me know what You want me to be a part of, and teach me to say no to those things that I should not give my time to. I press into Your presence for an encounter with You now. Just as Moses asked to see Your glory (Exodus 33:18), I too want to see Your glory. Speak to me face-to-face.

||||||||||||||||||||||||||||||||||||||||||||||||||||||||||||||||||||||

*The LORD would speak to Moses face
to face, as one speaks to a friend.*
EXODUS 33:11 NIV

In Christ

God, You have rescued me from the power of darkness and brought me into the kingdom of Your Son. Jesus paid the ultimate price to free me, and my sins are forgiven. Because of His great sacrifice, I am no longer separated from You. I can walk into Your presence without sin, fault, or blame. And so, I accept the gift given to me. I put on the truth of who I am in Christ. I am grateful to You for giving me new life. I turn my face toward the new. Eternity is now—and forever with You. I choose to live in Your truth today.

||||||||||||||||||||||||||||||||||||||||||||||||||||||||||||||||||||||||||||

He is the image of the invisible God,
the firstborn of all creation. . . . He existed
before everything and holds everything together.
COLOSSIANS 1:15, 17 GW

When to Remain Silent

Heavenly Father, Your Word says that the tongue has great power. My words can help or harm. There are times when silence is best. Help me to know the difference between times I should speak and times I should keep still. I pray for wisdom as I go through this day. I want my speech to honor You. Put a guard over my lips, I pray. Amen.

In the multitude of words there wanteth not sin: but he that refraineth his lips is wise.
PROVERBS 10:19 KJV

Spread God's Peace

Dear God, I pray for peace throughout the world, where there's so much pain, destruction, and disregard for Your creation. Some say peace is impossible—but with You all things are possible! Jesus declared peace for all Your children. We can never look to the world for true peace. That only comes from You. And although peace does not reign throughout the earth, it can reign in my heart. I can be a comfort to others in the middle of life's storms. Give me courage to speak life when things look dark. May Your peace be a tangible gift that I can share with others.

||||||||||||||||||||||||||||||||||||||||||||||||||||||||||||||||||||

"Peace I leave with you, My peace I give to you;
not as the world gives do I give to you. Let not
your heart be troubled, neither let it be afraid."
JOHN 14:27 NKJV

Soul Rest

Most of the time I'm not very good at doing nothing. Even when I put my feet up, my mind races with thoughts of what I could or should be doing. I need calm inactivity. I know I don't make it a priority like I should. But today I accept Your invitation, God, to experience a deeper intimacy with You through times of rest. Each day I will courageously step back, look at what I'm doing, and give You the opportunity to search my heart. Remind me to do this. Please refresh me now.

||||||||||||||||||||||||||||||||||||||||||||||||||||||||||||||||||||||||||

When the Lord has given you rest from your sorrow and pain and from your trouble and unrest and from the hard service with which you were made to serve. . . . The whole earth is at rest and is quiet; they break forth into singing.
ISAIAH 14:3, 7 AMPC

Holding on to His Promise

God, when You speak a word, it cannot return void. It always accomplishes what You send it to do. So when You make a promise, I believe it will definitely happen. The challenge is that time passes from when You give Your word to the end result. In that time I need to hold tightly to what You've said and not let doubt enter my mind or talk me out of what I believe You will do in my life. Help me stay strong and stand in faith. I will have courage! I trust that no matter how long it takes, it will be exactly as You've said. Your Word is forever true.

||||||||||||||||||||||||||||||||||||||||||||||||||||||||||||||||||||||||||||||

"So have courage, men! I trust God that
everything will turn out as he told me."
Acts 27:25 gw

You Make up the Difference

Lord, I'm feeling a little deficient as a parent today. I want to be my very best for my family. When I'm not, it hurts my heart and I feel guilty, but I know that's not what You want for me. Forgive me, and help me forgive myself. Be at work in my children's lives. I trust You to make up the difference when I misstep. Your love covers all. Show me how to parent with Your love. Give me confidence in my decisions. I am doing all I can to be the parent my children need. I look to You for guidance. Help me discipline when necessary and show grace when that is best.

||||||||||||||||||||||||||||||||||||||||||||||||||||||||||||||||||||||||||||||

Most important of all, continue to show deep love for each other, for love makes up for many of your faults.
1 PETER 4:8 TLB

Morning Comes
after the Storm

Father, You know the storms in my life, past and present. You know the one storm weighing heavily on my mind right now. The storm often feels stronger, more powerful, at night. My mind is flooded with negative thoughts, pouring in like ocean water that threatens to sink a ship. But You, my God, are my peace and my calm in the storm. I turn my face to You. I remember the times You took care of the storms of the past. Give me grace to navigate this storm as well. The morning will come and the storm will be no more. I rest in Your loving arms, safe and secure.

||||||||||||||||||||||||||||||||||||||||||||||||||||||||||||||||||||||||||||

Let the morning bring me word of your
unfailing love, for I have put my trust in you.
PSALM 143:8 NIV

Still Working on Me

Dear God, I'm a far cry from perfect, but I'm confident in the knowledge that You love me just as I am. You are the one who has begun a work in me, and You will be faithful to complete what has been started. What a thrill to know that You'll make me what You want me to be. Amen.

||||||||||||||||||||||||||||||||||||||||||||||||||||||||||||||||||||

Let not mercy and truth forsake thee: bind them about thy neck; write them upon the table of thine heart.
PROVERBS 3:3 KJV

Increase and Wealth

Father, as Your child, I want to be able to give to every good work. I want to be successful in business and fruitful. You have given me the ability to produce wealth. Lord, bless my work and make everything I put my hand to become a blessing in my life and in others' lives. I study Your Word to learn Your ways. I lean into Your Holy Spirit and receive Your wisdom so that I make good and godly choices. Lead me in the way I should go. Show me the path You've set before me to bring honor and glory to You in my profession.

||||||||||||||||||||||||||||||||||||||||||||||||||||||||||||||||||||||

But remember the LORD your God, for it is he who gives
you the ability to produce wealth, and so confirms his
covenant, which he swore to your ancestors, as it is today.
DEUTERONOMY 8:18 NIV

When I Need Strength

Father, I come to You today and ask for strength. I'm done relying on myself and placing my problems on others. I choose to step out of sadness and hurt into the joy only You give. From this joy comes the strength to finish my day and to get out of bed tomorrow. I can't find that anywhere else but Your presence.

Your daughters don't have to carry the stress of life alone. You give me the gift of the Holy Spirit. You ask me to come to You with all my burdens and doubts and promise to take these on Yourself. Thank You for that today. When I share my load with You, I can be more willing and open to do other tasks set before me.

||||||||||||||||||||||||||||||||||||||||||||||||||||||||||||||||||||||||||||

"Do not grieve, for the joy of the LORD is your strength."
NEHEMIAH 8:10 NIV

Great Faith

Why is it so hard to trust You sometimes? You have never failed me, and yet I struggle. I want to be full of faith. I want to accept every promise You make and believe they will happen for me, but sometimes I fear. Help me trust You. Help me have great faith. Today, I let go of my doubt. I surrender fully to You. Whatever is before me, I am determined to trust Your Word. You will not fail me. I can always count on You. You have said it, and I believe it. Help me continue to grow in faith.

|||||||||||||||||||||||||||||||||||||||||||||||||||||||||||||||||||||||||||

Jesus marveled at this. He turned around and said to the crowd who had followed him, "Listen, everyone! Never have I found among the people of God a man like this who believes so strongly in me."

LUKE 7:9 TPT

Shine the Light in My Community

There are dark forces at work in our schools, on our streets, and in our homes. I confront the enemy in the name of Jesus. Shine the light of Your glory and goodness into our community. Let Your light illuminate those who give way to evil. Let Your truth spring forth and eliminate the darkness. Protect and keep our first responders as they help us. Keep us safe from harm. You have overcome this world, Jesus. Give me the heart to intercede for others and the courage to protect the weak. Bring many of us believers together to stand against the darkness!

||||||||||||||||||||||||||||||||||||||||||||||||||||||||||||||||||||||||||

The night is far spent, the day is at hand. Therefore let us cast off the works of darkness, and let us put on the armor of light.
ROMANS 13:12 NKJV

Right Paths

The right path is often the one less traveled. I am learning this, Father, oh so slowly. You will always lead me in the right path. You will never lead me astray. I have been at the crossroads many times, and I will face such choices again and again. Keep my heart focused on You so that I might be led down pleasant paths, paths that will glorify my King. Amen.

||||||||||||||||||||||||||||||||||||||||||||||||||||||||||||||||||||||||

I have taught thee in the way of wisdom;
I have led thee in right paths.
PROVERBS 4:11 KJV

Staying Spiritually Fit

Heavenly Father, what I allow to go into my heart is important to You—and me. The things I think about make an impression on my soul. What I hear and see produces thoughts that lead to actions. Help me not to deceive myself by thinking I can rise above the negative input. I will be courageous and refuse to partake of things that I shouldn't. As I spend time in the Bible, thinking about who You are and what Your Word means, it fuels my faith. Help me stay faithful to growing in Your Word. Give me a deep desire to stay spiritually fit.

||||||||||||||||||||||||||||||||||||||||||||||||||||||||||||||||||||||

"Don't for a minute let this Book of The Revelation be out of mind. Ponder and meditate on it day and night, making sure you practice everything written in it. Then you'll get where you're going; then you'll succeed."
JOSHUA 1:8 MSG

Rejoice! Rejoice! Rejoice!

I celebrate Your goodness! I cheer and exalt You. I exclaim Your integrity and praise Your holy name. I rejoice over the miracles You have done and the many times You kept me from destruction. I thank You for the great works You are doing even now, and I celebrate all that You have yet to do in my life and the lives of those I love. You have given me Your unfailing Word; it cannot return void. It always accomplishes all that You send it to do. I will speak Your Word of truth and be glad. I will see Your goodness in the land of the living. It will be manifested before my eyes.

|||||||||||||||||||||||||||||||||||||||||||||||||||||||||||||||||||||||||

Rejoice in the Lord always [delight, gladden yourselves in Him]; again I say, Rejoice!
PHILIPPIANS 4:4 AMPC

Powerful Encourager

Lord, I am grateful for the wonderful community You've given me. I can count on them to be there for me when I need support. What a blessing to have authentic people to do life with! They speak life and grace into my life. And they also give me opportunity to do the same for them. Help me be a powerful encourager for others. Bring people across my path who need to hear Your Word. Speak to them through me. Help me be open to receive Your truth and wisdom from those You've placed in my life.

|||||||||||||||||||||||||||||||||||||||||||||||||||||||||||||||||||||||||||||||||||||||||||

Be merciful to those who doubt; save others by snatching them from the fire; to others show mercy, mixed with fear— hating even the clothing stained by corrupted flesh.
JUDE 22–23 NIV

God's Promise to Do Amazing Things

God, forgive me for my unbelief. Sometimes circumstances surround me and I am tempted to think You've forgotten me. But You would never abandon me. I remember the many times before when You rescued me. You showed up and delivered me. You've promised to do amazing things in my life. I am ready for a "suddenly"—a big surprise that will amaze me. I believe You will do abundantly above all I can ask or think. Help me wait with patience for Your timing. I praise You today, in advance, knowing something truly wonderful is on its way.

||||||||||||||||||||||||||||||||||||||||||||||||||||||||||||||||||||||||||||||

"Look at the nations and watch—and be utterly amazed. For I am going to do something in your days that you would not believe, even if you were told."
HABAKKUK 1:5 NIV

Hold on Tight

Lord, help me hold on tight to You. I don't want to miss a step, become deceived, or fall away. Let Your ways be made known to me. May they sink deeply into my understanding. It's not enough to hear Your desires for my life; I must focus my thoughts, my will, and my emotions in the right direction. Sometimes paying attention is hard work. I tune my spiritual ears to Your Word today. I will not just hear You but will also obey Your truths. I do not want to stray from Your plan. I desire to please You with all my heart.

|||||||||||||||||||||||||||||||||||||||||||||||||||||||||||||||||||||||||||||||

This is why it is so crucial that we be all the more engaged and attentive to the truths that we have heard so that we do not drift off course.
HEBREWS 2:1 TPT

Generosity

Father, the psalmist declares that he has never seen the righteous forsaken or his children going hungry. This inspires me. I know that You bless those who give. I want to leave a legacy of generosity for my children or for others who are influenced by my life. What they see me practicing regarding giving will impact their choices. May we be a generous family, always looking for opportunities to show mercy. Amen.

|||||||||||||||||||||||||||||||||||||||||||||||||||||||||||||||||||||||||

I have been young, and now am old; yet have I not seen
the righteous forsaken, nor his seed begging bread. He
is ever merciful, and lendeth; and his seed is blessed.
PSALM 37:25–26 KJV

Make Known What Is Right

Lord, You have not kept my purpose hidden from me. When I seek You for what is right, You let me know Your ways and Your desires. You are the Lord, and You speak the truth; You make known what is right. You have given me Your true Word. You have revealed the secrets for Your will in my life. I don't have to search for evidence that what You've said will come to pass. I see Your plans at work through changes every day. Thank You for sharing Your Word and making what is right known to me today.

I haven't spoken privately or in some dark corner of the world. I didn't say to Jacob's descendants, "Search for me in vain!" I, the LORD, speak what is fair and say what is right.
ISAIAH 45:19 GW

A Godly Friend

Lord, I want to be a better friend. Help me be trustworthy and devoted. Help me put the desires of my friends before my own. Give me the power of encouragement so that I may be at their side. Cleanse me and give me a pure heart. May my purity of heart flow out in gracious and encouraging words. May Your wisdom and peace speak life and love into the hearts of my friends. Let my lips bring joy and peace. I trust You, Lord, to help my words and actions point all my friends toward knowing and loving You.

|||||||||||||||||||||||||||||||||||||||||||||||||||||||||||||||||||||||||||

He who loves purity and the pure in heart and
who is gracious in speech—because of the grace
of his lips will he have the king for his friend.
PROVERBS 22:11 AMPC

God's Decree

God, I refuse to give up! I've been waiting, pressing in, asking and trusting that everything You've promised will occur. Thank You for the joy and the strength You've given me to endure this season. Thank You for the small things that are bringing about Your purpose and plans. I agree with Your Word. All that You've promised is on its way. Even now, I believe blessings are flowing into my life. Your goodness will overtake me. I give You praise today for the overflow.

||||||||||||||||||||||||||||||||||||||||||||||||||||||||||||||||||||||||||

"Things are going to happen so fast your head will swim, one thing fast on the heels of the other. You won't be able to keep up. Everything will be happening at once—and everywhere you look, blessings! Blessings like wine pouring off the mountains and hills."
AMOS 9:13 MSG

120

Belong to the God of the Living

Lord, You created me. You know my history and my future. You placed me on this earth to live a life pleasing to You, to know You and to serve You. No one else knows me like You do. I am grateful to be a part of Your family. I am thankful for all You've done in my life. I never have to wonder where I belong. I belong to You. You guide and direct me. Help me hear Your voice. Help me to always be in the right place at the right time to do Your will.

‖‖

"Don't you realize that God was speaking directly to you when he said, 'I am the God of Abraham, Isaac, and Jacob'? So God is not the God of the dead, but of the living."
MATTHEW 22:31–32 TLB

Perfecting Every Concern

Father, You know the weight I carry in my mind. You know all my thoughts. Help me rise above the thoughts that pervade my mind and influence my heart. Your mercy and love for me endure forever. They will never run out. You are at work in my life perfecting every single concern I have. You work all things out for my good. I turn my eyes to Your Word. I will put Your Word in my heart and trust You, that every word, every promise You have made will occur at the exact time You've purposed. I wait with patience.

The LORD will perfect that which concerns me;
Your mercy, O LORD, endures forever; do not
forsake the works of Your hands.
PSALM 138:8 NKJV

The Fruit

Lord, I'm not the perfect person I present to the world. There are certain times when I feel like I have to wear a disguise to get through my day. Only You, God, know the real me and accept me as I am. How can I throw away my false face and wear the crown that You give Your children? How can I show people not only the real me but the real You?

Thank You for giving us a list in Your Word of what we gain when we fully trust You. Instead of presenting who I think the world wants, let me show them a daughter who loves and is loved by You. I can do this by practicing the fruit of the Spirit, by diving into time with You. Thank You!

||||||||||||||||||||||||||||||||||||||||||||||||||||||||||||||||||||||

*But the fruit of the Spirit is love, joy, peace, forbearance,
kindness, goodness, faithfulness, gentleness and
self-control. Against such things there is no law.*
GALATIANS 5:22–23 NIV

A Woman Who
Fears the Lord

God, I want to be a Proverbs 31 woman. My focus should not be on external beauty or the clothing and jewelry that I wear. Rather, may others notice my heart that is forever seeking You. I want nothing more than to be known as a woman of God. Protect me from vanity. Outward beauty is not lasting, but a beautiful spirit is. I meditate upon Your Word now, Lord. I want to honor You. Amen.

||||||||||||||||||||||||||||||||||||||||||||||||||||||||||||||||||||||||||||||||

Favour is deceitful, and beauty is vain: but a woman that feareth the Lord, she shall be praised.
PROVERBS 31:30 KJV

For Loved Ones to Know

Jesus, it's difficult serving You when those I love most don't know You. I can't seem to make them understand. I want them to have a better life and assurance of eternal life in You. I don't want to argue or defend my relationship with You. Holy Spirit, lead me so that I know when to speak and when to be quiet. Help me choose words and actions that let them see You in me. I pray they see the difference You've made in my own life and will come to know You too. Bring someone into their life that they will listen to, if it's not me.

||||||||||||||||||||||||||||||||||||||||||||||||||||||||||||||||||||||||

Oh, the joys of those who do not follow evil men's advice, who do not hang around with sinners, scoffing at the things of God.
PSALM 1:1 TLB

God-Aligned Decisions

God, I want to make all my decisions according to Your will. Your way is the right way. Above all, I want to follow where You lead in my life. I need Your wisdom today. I have a hard decision to make. It's difficult because there seems to be no solution that won't hurt someone. Help me find the path that You want me to go on—even if it's the rockiest one. Prepare the hearts of those I need to speak with so that what You give me to say is received in the best possible way. Give me courage, Lord.

||||||||||||||||||||||||||||||||||||||||||||||||||||||||||||||||||||||||||||||||

I will praise and give thanks to You with uprightness of heart when I learn [by sanctified experiences] Your righteous judgments [Your decisions against and punishments for particular lines of thought and conduct].
PSALM 119:7 AMPC

Take the Land

God, You have given me the land. Your goodness and mercy have provided all I need. You told the Israelites to possess the land, and I too will take possession of everything You've given me. All Your promises are mine. I will follow Your instructions. Speak to my heart. Lead me according to Your promises. Show me the path to take and the words to say. Go before me and prepare the way. I refuse to be afraid or become discouraged no matter the challenges because You have given me victory. I take possession by faith and hold on tight.

|||||||||||||||||||||||||||||||||||||||||||||||||||||||||||||||||||||||||||||||||||

"The Lord God has given us this land. Go and possess it as he told us to. Don't be afraid! Don't even doubt!"
DEUTERONOMY 1:21 TLB

I Believe

Thank You for the stories in Your Word about people who struggled to believe. At times I struggle to believe. In my heart of hearts, I know You will deliver on Your promises. You never fail me, God. You are not a man; You cannot lie. But the weight of my troubles puts pressure on my soul. I fight the negative thoughts in my mind. I know I need to let go and not think about them, but continually I have to take those thoughts captive and replace them with Your Word. I need Your help! I will fill my heart with Your promises by reading Your promises. Help my unbelief.

||||||||||||||||||||||||||||||||||||||||||||||||||||||||||||||||||||||||||

Jesus said to him, "If you can believe, all things are possible to him who believes." Immediately the father of the child cried out and said with tears, "Lord, I believe; help my unbelief!"
MARK 9:23–24 NKJV

128

His Spirit in Me!

Thank You, Jesus, for my salvation. I never have to worry about whether I am really a Christian. No one can ever convince me otherwise. The same Spirit that raised You from the dead resides in me. That power is available to me, and I lean into it. The Holy Spirit is working within me. He helps me with daily challenges and teaches me to pray. I am empowered to serve God and do His will. I am a part of God's plan on the earth. His Spirit operates and flows through me even now.

|||||||||||||||||||||||||||||||||||||||||||||||||||||||||||||||||||||

And if the Spirit of him who raised Jesus from the dead is living in you, he who raised Christ from the dead will also give life to your mortal bodies because of his Spirit who lives in you.
ROMANS 8:11 NIV

Love My Family

Thank You for the relationships You've placed in my life. Show me the purpose of each one. Family is important to You, so it should be important to me. Sometimes family relationships are hard because of history or difficult personalities. Give me wisdom to know how to navigate the difficult relationships. Help me flow in Your love even when my emotions don't want to cooperate. I want to be a blessing to my family and not a hindrance. Help me relate to them as You desire. Above all, let me love them in a way that would make them want to know You.

||||||||||||||||||||||||||||||||||||||||||||||||||||||||||||||||||||||||||||||

Believe in the Lord Jesus Christ [give yourself up to Him, take yourself out of your own keeping and entrust yourself into His keeping] and you will be saved.
ACTS 16:31 AMPC

A Testimony

My life is a song of praise to You, my faithful Father, the giver of life! When people hear my testimony of Your goodness, may they come to know You. I want others to notice the difference in me and wonder why I have such joy, such peace. May I point them to You, Lord, and may they trust in You for salvation. You are the way, the truth, and the life. Amen.

||||||||||||||||||||||||||||||||||||||||||||||||||||||||||||||||||||||||||||||||

And he hath put a new song in my mouth, even praise unto our God: many shall see it, and fear, and shall trust in the LORD.
PSALM 40:3 KJV

Let My Life Shine

Heavenly Father, I want to let my light—the life that comes from You—shine before everyone. Create in me a clean heart, and cleanse me from all selfishness. My life will only shine if You are the source. I don't want to just get by, living a casual Christian life. I want my life to make a difference. Teach me to live and act in a way that speaks Your truth to others. Fill me with an undying passion to see lives changed for Your glory. When I'm called to defend my faith, help me do it in love, with gentleness and respect.

||||||||||||||||||||||||||||||||||||||||||||||||||||||||||||||||||||||||||||||

Light exposes the true character of everything because light makes everything easy to see. That's why it says: "Wake up, sleeper! Rise from the dead, and Christ will shine on you."
Ephesians 5:13–14 gw

Let Others See You in Me

Heavenly Father, today I build myself up in my most holy faith, praying in the Spirit as You speak to my heart. Help me recognize Your truth and turn away from the enemy's attempts to deceive me. Give me a spirit of discernment. Give me words to say in every situation so that I may be a witness to others of Your goodness and love. Thank You for Your power and strength to embrace those things that grow my faith. Let others see You in me today.

||||||||||||||||||||||||||||||||||||||||||||||||||||||||||||||||||||||

But you, dear friends, by building yourselves up in your most holy faith and praying in the Holy Spirit, keep yourselves in God's love as you wait for the mercy of our Lord Jesus Christ to bring you to eternal life.
JUDE 20–21 NIV

All Hope in Him

Today I place all my hope in You, God. I am learning that true peace can only come from You. I cannot depend on resting when a problem is resolved because often more problems are just around the corner. It does me no good to worry, so forgive me when I do. Help me stand firm in my confidence, knowing *You* are my hope. I am strong and courageous when I rest in Your holy hand. You work all things together for my good. Because of Your unfailing love, all power and authority belong to You. You have the final say regarding everything that concerns me. I will not let go of You. You are where my hope comes from.

||||||||||||||||||||||||||||||||||||||||||||||||||||||||||||||||||||||||||

"Power belongs to you, God,
and with you, Lord, is unfailing love."
PSALM 62:11–12 NIV

134

True Joy

I know that every person has individual battles. Many silently suffer through tough circumstances. May my life exude true joy from You. I don't want to pretend or deny what I'm going through, but not everyone needs to know what's going on with me. Help me share Your joy with others, bringing positivity and encouragement. Thank You for those close friends that I trust to share my struggles with. Remind me to also lend a hand and give support to them in their time of need. I want to be a heart with ears so that I can help them navigate life with joy. May I bring healing to those around me, always.

|||||||||||||||||||||||||||||||||||||||||||||||||||||||||||||||||||||

A cheerful heart does good like medicine,
but a broken spirit makes one sick.
PROVERBS 17:22 TLB

Christlike Relationships

God, I am grateful to belong to You—to be Your child. Even more, I am thankful for my brothers and sisters in Christ that You have brought into my life. May I be a voice of encouragement to each of them. May Your words be my words when I speak into their lives as You inspire me to do so. May I speak with Your love, mercy, and grace. Give me ears to hear Your heart as You lead our conversations. May all my children—spiritual or natural—live according to Your truth. May we bring glory to You in our relationships.

|||||||||||||||||||||||||||||||||||||||||||||||||||||||||||||||||||||||||||

It is the greatest joy of my life to hear that my children
are consistently living their lives in the ways of truth!
3 JOHN 4 TPT

The Day of Salvation

Father, waiting to live until my circumstances change is no way to live. I need to live now and enjoy the moments You've given me. I will live each day with thanksgiving and hope, knowing You are always at work; You are doing what is necessary to bring Your promises into my life at just the right time. *Now* is the right time to expect and experience Your saving grace, mercy, and love. You have answered me with a sure salvation. You have restored me and responded to me with an unbreakable promise.

|||||||||||||||||||||||||||||||||||||||||||||||||||||||||||||||||||||

For he says, I listened to you at the time of my favor.
And the day when you needed salvation, I came
to your aid. So can't you see? Now is the time to
respond to his favor! Now is the day of salvation!
2 CORINTHIANS 6:2 TPT

Faith Always Produces

God, I look back at where I've been as I'm facing another trial, and I see that You've been faithful. As I trust You now, I know that You have a plan. You always bring me through. Help me not to grow tired. Honestly, sometimes I do want to give up. But then where would I be? I'd be stuck. I cannot quit. I must press on. You are my hope. You will deliver me from this hardship. I will eventually come out on the other side, as long as I hold on to You. My faith in You always produces Your very best for me because You love me and You will never fail me.

||||||||||||||||||||||||||||||||||||||||||||||||||||||||||||||||||||||||||

Consider it pure joy, my brothers and sisters, whenever you face trials of many kinds, because you know that the testing of your faith produces perseverance.
JAMES 1:2–3 NIV

Blessing Those
Who Hurt You

God, when someone hurts me, I don't feel like blessing him or her. Remind me what Your Word teaches about love. Love keeps no record of wrongs. Love forgives. It restores. Love tries again. Love lets it go. Love blesses even when it's not my turn to bless! Give me a spirit of love that trumps evil. And allow me to bless those who hurt me. I can only do so in Your power. Amen.

||||||||||||||||||||||||||||||||||||||||||||||||||||||||||||||||||||||||||

Not rendering evil for evil, or railing for railing:
but contrariwise blessing; knowing that ye are
thereunto called, that ye should inherit a blessing.
1 PETER 3:9 KJV

Cheers to Giving

God, You are a generous giver. Your Word says You will provide seed to the sower and in due season I will reap a harvest. Thank You for the seed I've sown and for the harvest that is on the way. I realize what I have to give goes far beyond financial gifts. Open my eyes to any opportunity You set before me to give cheerfully. I appreciate each opportunity to be generous. Show me the many different ways You would have me give into the lives of others. Just as You meet all my needs, may I remain openhanded, ready to help others in every way I can.

||||||||||||||||||||||||||||||||||||||||||||||||||||||||||||||||||||||||

Each of you should give whatever you have decided.
You shouldn't be sorry that you gave or feel forced
to give, since God loves a cheerful giver.
2 Corinthians 9:7 GW

Big-Picture Focus

Lord, each day that I have breath in my lungs is a gift from You. Forgive me for the times when my perspective has been on the problems I face. Help me make every minute count. Help me step back and enjoy the precious times You give me, with You and with those I love. Give me a big-picture focus. Let me look deeply at the things that really matter and gloss over those that don't. Reveal to me the things that I need to know by Your Spirit.

"Eye has not seen, nor ear heard, nor have entered into the heart of man the things which God has prepared for those who love Him." But God has revealed them to us through His Spirit. For the Spirit searches all things, yes, the deep things of God.
1 CORINTHIANS 2:9–10 NKJV

Living a God-Fashioned Life

You know I have struggled to put the past behind me. My old nature, before Christ, still tries to hold on to me. I no longer want that life. You have made me new. And I want, more than anything, to live my life fashioned after You. Thank You for seeing me as that new creature. I will become a person who accurately represents You. Give me courage to give up the excuses and get rid of what doesn't please You. Today, I take off the old and walk away.

That old way of life has to go. It's rotten through and through. Get rid of it! And then take on an entirely new way of life—a God-fashioned life, a life renewed from the inside and working itself into your conduct as God accurately reproduces his character in you.
EPHESIANS 4:22–24 MSG

Confidence in Prayer

Father, thank You for Jesus. I know that because of faith in Him, I have access to the presence of God every second of the day. I am never alone. I know with complete trust that You'll answer my prayer. And I know that to pray confidently, I have to come to You with open hands and an open heart, willing to listen to what You have to say. Even if that includes something I don't want to hear.

I know that the key to confident prayer is praising Your name, confessing my sins, and aligning my will with Yours. When I pray, help me to recognize when I take my eyes off You. My first priority is following You and not my own desires. Thank You for being there.

||||||||||||||||||||||||||||||||||||||||||||||||||||||||||||||||||||||||

*Let us draw near to God with a sincere heart and
with the full assurance that faith brings, having our
hearts sprinkled to cleanse us from a guilty conscience
and having our bodies washed with pure water.*
HEBREWS 10:22 NIV

Placing the Puzzle Pieces

With strong assurance, I know that You are my partner in this plan You have for me. Thank You for Your promise that all things work together for my good. Your plan is like a big puzzle, but I don't have a picture of what that puzzle looks like when it's finished. So as I put the pieces together, lead me through the work. I trust You to put the pieces in the right places so that when it is finished, my life looks exactly the way You have envisioned it. I hold tightly to Your hand and follow Your specific direction today.

|||||||||||||||||||||||||||||||||||||||||||||||||||||||||||||||||||||||||||

We are assured and know that [God being a partner in their labor] all things work together and are [fitting into a plan] for good to and for those who love God and are called according to [His] design and purpose.
ROMANS 8:28 AMPC

A Thankful Heart

Lord, everything good in my life comes from You. Often I forget to thank You. I am thankful for Your provision and Your protection. I am thankful for my family and friends. I am most of all thankful for the joy of my salvation, which comes through Christ. Give me a grateful heart, I pray. Let me always remember that every good and perfect gift comes from Your hand. Amen.

||||||||||||||||||||||||||||||||||||||||||||||||||||||||||||||||||||||

*And let the peace of God rule in your hearts, to the which
also ye are called in one body; and be ye thankful.*
COLOSSIANS 3:15 KJV

I Can Never Be Forgotten

Praise You, God! You will never abandon me. You cannot forget me! No matter how I feel or what crazy thoughts run through my head, I belong to You. I refuse to be moved by my emotions because they always fail me. I am Your covenant child. I hold tightly to that truth. You will never forsake me. When I feel lost or alone, I imagine Your hand with who I am to You engraved deeply into Your palm. You will never lose sight of me. I remain constantly on Your mind and in Your view. My relationship with You is the reality. I am holding tightly to Your promises, believing Your truth.

||||||||||||||||||||||||||||||||||||||||||||||||||||||||||||||||||||||||

I have engraved you on the palms of my hands.
Your walls are always in my presence.
ISAIAH 49:16 GW

I Trust You

So many things have happened in my life that I don't understand. I've been angry, been frightened, and wanted answers. But today I choose to trust You, Lord. With all my heart I choose to acknowledge You. You know what You're doing. My life is in Your hands. I don't have to know why. I want the details, but if You decide I don't need them, then I submit to You. I let go of it all. Courageously, I step out in faith, believing You are leading me toward the best outcome. You will show me the way to go, and I am determined to follow You.

|||||||||||||||||||||||||||||||||||||||||||||||||||||||||||||||||||||||||

Trust in the LORD with all your heart and lean not on your own understanding; in all your ways submit to him, and he will make your paths straight.
PROVERBS 3:5–6 NIV

I Love You,
Forever and Always

Lord, I love You. You shield and defend me from the seen and the unseen. When circumstances suddenly go a different direction than I thought, I trust that You have prevented a more terrible thing from coming into my life. When I think I have no more strength for the struggle at hand, You become my strength. You are my Defender and my Deliverer. You pull me out of the mess. You are my salvation. You continually save me from anything I need to be saved from. I rest in Your arms. No matter what comes, I love You forever and always.

The Lord is my Rock, my Fortress, and my Deliverer;
my God, my keen and firm Strength in Whom
I will trust and take refuge, my Shield, and the
Horn of my salvation, my High Tower.
PSALM 18:2 AMPC

No More in Darkness

Heavenly Father, I no longer live in fear of the darkness. Endless nighttimes are no longer my companion. I am grateful that I can now reside in the freedom of Your glorious light. Through Christ, You have opened the door for me to share in His inheritance. You have given me every spiritual blessing. You rescued me from the devil's dominion and adopted me as Your very own child. You planted me inside Your eternal kingdom, forgave all my sins, and redeemed me from any judgment. Thank You for all I have in Christ. He is the truth, the way, and the light!

|||||||||||||||||||||||||||||||||||||||||||||||||||||||||||||||||||||||||||

God has rescued us from the power of darkness and has brought us into the kingdom of his Son, whom he loves.
COLOSSIANS 1:13 GW

Special to the Father

How can I doubt my worth in Your eyes, Father? You know the number of hairs on my head. You created me, and You said that Your creation is very good. When I'm tempted to get down on myself, remind me that I am special to You, and there's no one just like me. Amen.

||||||||||||||||||||||||||||||||||||||||||||||||||||||||||||||||||||

*In the multitude of my thoughts within
me thy comforts delight my soul.*
PSALM 94:19 KJV

Lord, Help!

It's the simplest prayer, Lord, and I don't say it nearly enough. I was created to need Your assistance. I should always look to You to provide the answers I need, but sometimes I don't. Forgive me when I look to others for the answers You alone can provide. Remind me that the solution is always in my best interest when I ask You. You always wait patiently for me to ask. I know I'm sometimes slow in doing so. Help me not to lean on my own understanding or try to work things out on my own but to always reach out to You. You have promised, and today I'm asking for Your help.

||||||||||||||||||||||||||||||||||||||||||||||||||||||||||||||||||||||||

"For I am the Lord your God who takes hold of your right hand and says to you, Do not fear; I will help you."
ISAIAH 41:13 NIV

Going Forth,
Stronger than Before

Lord, I am standing in the middle of transition. Many things that used to be are no longer so. It's time for me to lead myself and others in a forward motion. Although my responsibilities are changing, I am not without help. You've provided the training and preparation. I have all I need. You have placed me on a firm foundation. I am ready to go forth, building on what I've learned, moving on stronger than before. When I am uncertain, remind me to look back at the experiences You've given me. I will draw wisdom from my journey so far.

||||||||||||||||||||||||||||||||||||||||||||||||||||||||||||||||||||||

*Hold tightly to the pattern of truth I
taught you, especially concerning the
faith and love Christ Jesus offers you.*
2 TIMOTHY 1:13 TLB

Holy Invitation

God, You are a holy fire, roaring through the forest, consuming everything in Your way. You cannot be contained. I invite Your Holy Spirit to burn through me, devouring everything that is worthless and sinful. Create in me a pure heart and let only what is good and dedicated to You remain. I let go of the things that keep me imprisoned, like selfishness, insecurity, pride, and envy. You are filled with compassion. Your love saved me from sin and death. Give me a desire to see others set free. Ignite my heart, and fuel a passion in my soul to do the things You've asked me to do. Set things in motion today that will help me achieve the dream You've given me.

|||||||||||||||||||||||||||||||||||||||||||||||||||||||||||||||||||||||||||

For our God is a holy, devouring fire!
HEBREWS 12:29 TPT

Blessed Assurance

Heavenly Father, my salvation is a gift—something I could never earn, but a treasure given freely with no strings attached. It is mine and can never be taken from me. Nothing can separate me from Your love. Forgive me for the times that I doubted my salvation or thought it was something I needed to achieve or win. Thank You for believing in me, trusting me with Your love. I can stand in confidence each day, knowing that I am saved and that I belong to You. My salvation is assured.

|||||||||||||||||||||||||||||||||||||||||||||||||||||||||||||||||||||||||||||||||

And by this we know that we are of the truth, and shall assure our hearts before Him. For if our heart condemns us, God is greater than our heart, and knows all things. Beloved, if our heart does not condemn us, we have confidence toward God.
1 JOHN 3:19–21 NKJV

The Answer Is on the Way

Lord, You know my prayer requests before they ever cross my lips, and yet, I know You desire for me to ask. So today, I am asking You to perfect those things that weigh heavily on my heart and mind. I trust that You have already started working behind the scenes on my behalf. You know the details and how they should work out best for me. The answer I need, whether I know it's what I need or not, is on its way. Help me patiently wait for Your perfect work to be perfected in my situation.

"The moment you began praying a command was given. I am here to tell you what it was, for God loves you very much. Listen and try to understand the meaning of the vision that you saw!"

DANIEL 9:23 TLB

Freed from Death

I take courage today knowing I belong to the one who raised Christ from the dead. All power and dominion belong to You. Because of Your willingness to give Your one and only Son, and His willingness to die for me, I have the opportunity to live my life in You. You have given me eternal life. I am forever restored to relationship with You. And eternity begins now. I don't have to wait for heaven; I have forever to spend with You. Death could not hold Jesus, and it cannot hold me. I have been freed from the grave.

"But God raised him from the dead, freeing him from the agony of death, because it was impossible for death to keep its hold on him."

Getting Older

Lord, I find myself reaching for what used to be. I tell myself that it was easier and better in my past and that age has only brought hardship. Why can't I go back to who I was? Where is that girl that trusted You so openly?

I know, Father, that You're the one who turns the seasons. I am where I am because You have found it important for me to be here. My age doesn't matter when I look at the eternity I get to spend with You.

I'm confident that every change to my body and circumstances has been ordained in Your will. I embrace the wisdom I have gained over the years, the scars and marks that led me closer to You. When I look at my life as a testament to You, I can embrace who I am.

||||||||||||||||||||||||||||||||||||||||||||||||||||||||||||||||||||||||||

Do not say, "Why were the old days better than these?" For it is not wise to ask such questions.
ECCLESIASTES 7:10 NIV

Love Covers Sins

Lord, all of my sin was nailed to the cross when Your Son died for me. Without grace, I am but filthy rags before a holy God. But through Christ, I am adopted as Your daughter, forgiven. There is pride in this daughter, God. Pride that resists forgiveness. Pride that says "I am right." Remind me of the multitude of my own sins that Your love covered through Jesus. Help me to love others well. Amen.

|||||||||||||||||||||||||||||||||||||||||||||||||||||||||||||||||||||||||

Hatred stirreth up strifes: but love covereth all sins.
PROVERBS 10:12 KJV

Never Anxious

When I'm tempted to allow my thoughts to pull me under the waters of anxiety, remind me that You never want me to be anxious about anything. I don't need to be worried. Today I spend time saturating my soul in prayer. Help me offer up faith-filled requests to You throughout the day. I will overflow with gratitude and thanksgiving. Thank You that I can share every detail of my life with You, knowing I won't be condemned or judged but comforted. Thank You for Your wonderful peace that surpasses my own human understanding. Thank You for an immediate inner calm in my heart. When my soul is anxious, I will hold tightly to Your promise of peace.

*Be anxious for nothing, but in everything by
prayer and supplication, with thanksgiving,
let your requests be made known to God.*
PHILIPPIANS 4:6 NKJV

Astonishingly Blessed

Heavenly Father, You have poured, are pouring, and will continue to pour out Your power in my life in astonishing ways. I am always ready for anything and everything. Because You prepare me, I am more than ready to do what needs to be done. Whatever I need, I can count on You to go above and beyond. You give freely. Your right-living, right-giving ways never run out. Thank You for Your astonishing blessings in my life every day.

||||||||||||||||||||||||||||||||||||||||||||||||||||||||||||||||||||||||||||||||

And God is able to make all grace (every favor and earthly blessing) come to you in abundance, so that you may always and under all circumstances and whatever the need be self-sufficient [possessing enough to require no aid or support and furnished in abundance for every good work and charitable donation].
2 CORINTHIANS 9:8 AMPC

His Favor, Always

Heavenly Father, because I am Your child, I am blessed. Pour out Your favor on me. Forgive me for the times You've prepared a blessing and I got in the way. Forgive me for trying to make things happen all by myself—in my timing instead of Yours. Give me ears to hear wisdom when You speak. I will listen to those You've placed in my life to mentor me. I choose to be pliable and moldable; I don't want to be stiff and inflexible to Your will. I choose Your way and not my own. My plans are big, but in no way do they compare to Yours. You saved me. May Your favor rest on me all the days of my life.

||||||||||||||||||||||||||||||||||||||||||||||||||||||||||||||||||||||||||||

And Esther obtained favor in the sight of all who saw her.
ESTHER 2:15 NKJV

Life Everlasting

I get lost in the busyness of life sometimes—a lot of the time—and forget that I am not of this world. My future is eternal. Help me remember what is important. Things of this life fade away when compared to eternity with You. Remind me to build up my treasure in heaven; this world is just a place I'm passing through. I am most thankful for everlasting life. Give me opportunities to share this truth. Give me words to speak as You stir hearts to receive this gift. May my life lead others to You.

||||||||||||||||||||||||||||||||||||||||||||||||||||||||||||||||||||||||||||

"For here is the way God loved the world—he gave his only, unique Son as a gift. So now everyone who believes in him will never perish but experience everlasting life."

JOHN 3:16 TPT

Boldness to Go

Heavenly Father, You have great plans for me, and I don't want to miss one single thing. Today I set my heart in alignment with Your will. I will obediently answer Your call and willingly do what You ask. Bring people across my path who will join with me in Your purposes, and help me know who they are. Give me boldness to do whatever You ask. I am determined to stay focused on You. I will not be deterred. Prepare me for the things ahead. Direct my path, and help me move forward when You say, "Go!" Clear the path before me.

|||||||||||||||||||||||||||||||||||||||||||||||||||||||||||||||||||||||||||

*Paul. . .welcomed all who visited him, telling them with
all boldness about the Kingdom of God and about the
Lord Jesus Christ; and no one tried to stop him.*
ACTS 28:30–31 TLB

163

Listening to God's Direction

Father, thank You for Your wisdom. I've not always taken the time to ask You which way to go before moving forward, or even if I did ask, sometimes I didn't wait patiently for an answer. I desire Your will for my life. I want to be in the right place at the right time. May I move with You, forever listening for Your voice for direction. Show me the way I should go. Speak to me when I've gone off on my own. Bring me back to the place of peace— a place I can only find in You. Your ways are not my ways. Help me to always choose Your path for my life.

||||||||||||||||||||||||||||||||||||||||||||||||||||||||||||||||||||||||||

Whether you turn to the right or to the left, your ears will hear a voice behind you, saying, "This is the way; walk in it."
ISAIAH 30:21 NIV

Comfort during Loss

Jesus, You know my sorrow, my grief, my pain. No one truly understands my heart—but You. I have a lot of questions I want to know the answers to, and perhaps those answers can only come from You. Show me the path that is right, because sometimes I am blinded by my grief. Hold me tight as I let the tears fall. Wash away the brokenness. Help me let go of the pain and say goodbye to all the hurts. Fill me with Your peace.

|||||||||||||||||||||||||||||||||||||||||||||||||||||||||||||||||||||||||||||

Blessed be the God and Father of our Lord Jesus Christ,
the Father of mercies and God of all comfort, who
comforts us in all our tribulation, that we may be able to
comfort those who are in any trouble, with the comfort
with which we ourselves are comforted by God.
2 CORINTHIANS 1:3–4 NKJV

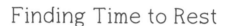

Finding Time to Rest

I find it difficult to even sit down to a meal, Father. Resting seems like such a far-fetched notion. I know You want me to find time to rest and spend time with You, but I'm on the go constantly, and I still don't get everything done. Please help me, Lord, to make resting a priority. Amen.

Cast thy burden upon the LORD, and he shall sustain thee: he shall never suffer the righteous to be moved.
PSALM 55:22 KJV

Always with Me

Fear comes like a dark shadow to engulf me, but I refuse to become fear's prisoner. As the waves of doubt and unbelief try to wash me away, I remind myself that You are always with me. You are my hope, my light, my salvation. You shine Your life into my situation. You bring peace into my heart and settle me. You speak courage and I draw strength from Your words. I am comforted by Your presence, and the storm around me roars no more. Fill me with Your peace now.

|||||||||||||||||||||||||||||||||||||||||||||||||||||||||||||||||||||||||||||

Immediately he spoke to them and said, "Take courage! It is I. Don't be afraid." Then he climbed into the boat with them, and the wind died down. They were completely amazed.
MARK 6:50–51 NIV

Follow Close to You

Lord, I live in a messed-up world. When bad things happen to good people, it's difficult for me to understand. I know that You hold my life in Your hands. My time is not my own, but Yours, and yet I desire a long life filled with Your goodness and love. Forgive me for the times I've closed off areas of my heart to You. I open them wide. When I call, You always answer. When I feel like I'm fighting a battle alone, give me assurance that You are with me. I will follow close to You. Hide me from my enemies, and keep me in safety next to You.

||||||||||||||||||||||||||||||||||||||||||||||||||||||||||||||||||||||||||

Yes, Lord, help us against our enemies, for man's help is useless. With God's help we shall do mighty things, for he will trample down our foes.
PSALM 60:11–12 TLB

Rejection

God, help me to remember that when I feel rejected, I'm in very good company. Your Son was sent to this earth and rejected by the ones He died for. It gives me comfort to know that my Creator understands my pain and grieves with me through this hurt.

This rejection is leading me closer to the purpose You have given me. I can choose to wallow in this and let it hinder Your plans, or I can keep moving forward with the grace and dignity that You supply to all Your daughters. You don't call us to stay in anger or hurt but to take everything with an understanding that there is more than what this world can give us. Thank You for this protection.

I will keep my gaze set on You and follow Your will above all.

||||||||||||||||||||||||||||||||||||||||||||||||||||||||||||||||||||||||||

The stone the builders rejected has become the cornerstone.
PSALM 118:22 NIV

169

Unshakable

When the earth moves beneath me because of the circumstances of my life, I look to You, Lord. When hope threatens to escape me, You are the one I hold on to. You are my stability and strength. My heart will remain steady despite all I see. I turn my eyes to You. I look up because You are my light and my salvation. When opposition raises its head against me, I refuse to fear. It cannot hold me within its prison bars. I remain free and unshakable because You hold me in the palm of Your hand.

My heart will not fear even if an army rises to attack.
I will not be shaken, even if war is imminent.
PSALM 27:3 TPT

Revive My Soul

God, I don't want to miss anything You have for me. I want to know You more. I want to go deeper in my relationship with You. Stir up Your life in me. Give me a desire for revitalization in my soul. Help me recognize distractions that keep me from reaching those goals You want me to reach. Show me how to speak life to others in a way that points them to You. Fill me with a passion for Your kingdom. Speak to me. Guide me. I want to be used for Your glory. May all I do bring You pleasure all the days of my life.

||||||||||||||||||||||||||||||||||||||||||||||||||||||||||||||||||||||

Revive us, and we will call upon Your name. Restore us, O Lord God of hosts; cause Your face to shine, and we shall be saved!
PSALM 80:18–19 NKJV

With Me through the Fire

Lord, You told us in Your Word to expect difficulty in this life. Your Word is full of miracles where You protected those You loved. I think of how You stood in the fire with Shadrach, Meshach, and Abednego. The fire was so hot that the people who threw them into it died, and yet they walked out without smelling like smoke. I cling tightly to Your promise today that when I go through the fire, I will not be burned up. The flames cannot consume me because You are with me. I will emerge from this circumstance, and I won't even smell like smoke. Thank You, Lord!

||||||||||||||||||||||||||||||||||||||||||||||||||||||||||||||||||||||||||

When you walk through the fire of oppression, you will not be burned up—the flames will not consume you.
ISAIAH 43:2 TLB

Showing That I Love God

How do I show that I love You, God? It must be more than merely a phrase I use in prayer. The way I show it is to keep Your commandments. I need Your strength for this. I fail every day. Renew my desire to live according to Your principles. They are not suggestions. They are commands. Honoring them will cause me to see You at work in my life. I love You, Lord. Amen.

||||||||||||||||||||||||||||||||||||||||||||||||||||||||||||||||||||||

He that hath my commandments, and keepeth them, he it is that loveth me: and he that loveth me shall be loved of my Father, and I will love him, and will manifest myself to him.
JOHN 14:21 KJV

My Deliverance

You are my deliverer. The heavy weight of life's challenges brings me to my knees, at the throne of Your grace. Thoughts of defeat overwhelm me, and yet I remember the Israelites standing between the Egyptians and the Red Sea. Their oppressors were closing in fast, and fear of returning to captivity pressed in. Miraculously, You parted the sea and made a way of escape for them. You will do the same for me. Nothing is impossible for You. You will show me the way out in Your time. I trust that my deliverance is on its way.

|||||||||||||||||||||||||||||||||||||||||||||||||||||||||||||||||||||||||||||||||||

Moses spoke to the people: "Don't be afraid. Stand firm and watch God do his work of salvation for you today. Take a good look at the Egyptians today for you're never going to see them again."
EXODUS 14:13 MSG

With Gratitude

You have been with me from the beginning, Lord. You have kept my foot from slipping and lifted me out of deep pits. You hold me up when the world falls away before me. You have hidden me from my enemies. You have saved the lives of my family. Forgive me for my complaints. I will never forget Your hand on my life. Thank You for the times You've turned things around and made a way when I could see no way. You have brought me this far, and with gratitude from deep in my heart, I thank You!

||||||||||||||||||||||||||||||||||||||||||||||||||||||||||||||||||

Then King David went in and sat before the LORD, and he said: "Who am I, Sovereign LORD, and what is my family, that you have brought me this far?"
2 SAMUEL 7:18 NIV

To Honor the Lord in My Relationships

Lord, I pray for believers. I am part of the body of Christ. May we live in fellowship with You and with one another. May we come together in unity. Show me today how I can strengthen my connection with fellow believers and serve them. Help me use my gifts to build others up in faith. Give me words of wisdom and a heart of understanding to work with my brothers and sisters in Christ in a way that pleases You. Thank You for divine relationships. Thank You for those You've called to be a part of my life and my destiny. May I always honor You in my relationships.

||||||||||||||||||||||||||||||||||||||||||||||||||||||||||||||||||||||||||

Don't you realize that together you have become
God's inner sanctuary and that the Spirit of
God makes his permanent home in you?
1 CORINTHIANS 3:16 TPT

Amazing Grace

Lord, I get so caught up in trying to do good works sometimes. I need to remember that I am saved by grace. You are pleased with me simply because I believe in Your Son, Jesus, and I have accepted Him as my Savior. You do not bless me or withhold good gifts based on my performance. Remind me of Your amazing grace, and make me gracious with others. In Jesus' name I pray, amen.

||||||||||||||||||||||||||||||||||||||||||||||||||||||||||||||||||||

For by grace are ye saved through faith;
and that not of yourselves: it is the gift of God:
not of works, lest any man should boast.
Ephesians 2:8–9 kjv

Grace for Everything

Father, I'm thankful for Your grace—Your unmerited favor to me through Jesus Christ, and that special strength You give Your child in times of need, trial, and temptation. If not for Your grace, I wouldn't even be able to approach You. Thank You for extending favor to me: forgiving my sins and adopting me into Your family. And thank You so much for that extra dose of perseverance that You keep giving to me in tough situations. I'm so thankful Your resources will never run short. I praise You today for grace. Amen.

||||||||||||||||||||||||||||||||||||||||||||||||||||||||||||||||||||

But he gives us more grace.
JAMES 4:6 NIV

My Work Is a Joy

Lord, You have given me talents and gifts, and I desire to use them for Your glory. Thank You for giving me work to do and for blessing the work of my hands. Help me be diligent in whatever You put before me. May I work earnestly, with honor and integrity. Give me joy as I work because I do everything as unto You. Sometimes work is harder than I expected. Sometimes there are things that seem unfair. Help me remember that You've placed me exactly where You want me. Thank You for the opportunity to touch others with my life. May all I do bring them closer in relationship with You.

||||||||||||||||||||||||||||||||||||||||||||||||||||||||||||||||||||||||||

Whatever your hand finds to do,
do it with all your might.
ECCLESIASTES 9:10 NIV

Undeniable Love

Father, You are love personified. Everything You do is out of love. You loved me so much You gave Your one and only Son as a sacrifice so I could have a relationship with You. Thank You for choosing to love me unconditionally. May the undeniable love You've shown me be evident in my life. Let the Holy Spirit empower me to show Your love. Help me see love as a choice and not an emotional response. I desire to live my life poured out for others, demonstrating Your love to them in every word and deed.

||||||||||||||||||||||||||||||||||||||||||||||||||||||||||||||||||||||||

In this the love of God was made manifest (displayed)
where we are concerned: in that God sent His
Son, the only begotten or unique [Son], into the
world so that we might live through Him.
1 John 4:9 ampc

Keeping Faith

Father, let me remember that the amount of my faith in You isn't a matter of when but a matter of now. All the faith I need to trust Your plan, to be confident in who You made me to be, and to be secure in my salvation is already inside of me.

I don't have to wait to gain the faith that I read about from the heroes of the Bible or that I see in the leaders around me. I have their exact same faith from the exact same God. I'm just as special to You as they are, Lord. And You have also created an amazing purpose for me as well!

I will step into that purpose today, God, with complete faith in You.

|||||||||||||||||||||||||||||||||||||||||||||||||||||||||||||||||||||||||||

Let love and faithfulness never leave you; bind them around your neck, write them on the tablet of your heart.
PROVERBS 3:3 NIV

Steward of Grace

Thank You for the gifts You have given me, Lord. I look around at the other believers in my life. We are all gifted in different ways. Help me to be a good steward of the gifts You have entrusted me with in this life. Instead of looking out for myself, may I have opportunities to use my abilities to minister to others. I understand that it is in doing so that I honor You. Amen.

As every man hath received the gift, even so minister the same one to another, as good stewards of the manifold grace of God.
1 PETER 4:10 KJV

Always Listening

Lord, You are always with me. You are my audience of one. You never miss a single thing. I know for certain that You always hear me. Even when I feel alone and Your voice is difficult to hear because of the noise in this busy world, You are listening. Never let me believe the lie that You don't care. I love You and You love me. I trust that You are always working on my behalf. You have my best interests at heart. You bring all things together for my good in Your perfect time.

|||||||||||||||||||||||||||||||||||||||||||||||||||||||||||||||||||||||||||

I am passionately in love with God because he listens to me. He hears my prayers and answers them.
PSALM 116:1 TPT

Seasons of Life

Jesus, You said this world is not without trouble. I am not exempt from the highs and lows, the mountains and valleys, so I will walk by faith and not by my feelings. May I always be thankful for all the seasons in life. May I praise You and rejoice when things are going well but even more so when there's difficulty and pain. Help me keep my focus on You, Lord. When the winter becomes unbearable or the summers of life grow uncomfortably hot, I will remember that nothing lasts forever. You are leading me, even when I cannot see what's next. By faith, I will follow You.

||||||||||||||||||||||||||||||||||||||||||||||||||||||||||||||||||||||||||||

Everything is appropriate in its own time. But though God has planted eternity in the hearts of men, even so, many cannot see the whole scope of God's work from beginning to end.
ECCLESIASTES 3:11 TLB

An Heir to the King

Heavenly Father, thank You for adopting me as an heir to the King of kings! You provided a way for me to come before You, Holy God. Christ carried my sin as His burden. It was nailed to the cross and has been forgiven forever, once and for all. Thank You for the abundant life that is mine because I am Yours. I praise You for viewing me through a lens called grace. Amen.

||||||||||||||||||||||||||||||||||||||||||||||||||||||||||||||||||||||||||

That being justified by his grace, we should be
made heirs according to the hope of eternal life.
TITUS 3:7 KJV

Scripture Index

OLD TESTAMENT